ARABS&ISRAEL

FOR BEGINNERS

BY RON DAVID
ILLUSTRATED BY SUSAN DAVID

Writers and Readers

WRITERS AND READERS PUBLISHING, INCORPORATED
P.O. Box 461, Village Station
New York, New York 10014

c/o Airlift Book Company
8, The Arena
Mollison Avenue
Enfield, EN3 7NJ
England

A Writers and Readers Documentary Comic Book
Copyright © 1993
Library of Congress Catalog Card Number:
ISBN#: 0-86316-161-8
 2 3 4 5 6 7 8 9 0

Manufactured in the United States of America

Beginners Documentary Comic Books are published by Writers and Readers Publishing, Inc. Its trademark, consisting of the words "For Beginners, Writers and Readers Documentary Comic Books" and Writers and Readers logo, is registered in the U.S. Patent and Trademark Office and in other countries.

ARABS&ISRAEL
FOR BEGINNERS

Writers and Readers

For my father.

We miss you.
But at the same time
We feel a little sorry for God.

I don't think you'd like this book.
But you'd be proud of me for writing it.
Thanks for everything.

CONTENTS

INTRODUCTION

Where Is this Book Heading?

Suave Lies

A writer who strings you along for 150 pages before telling you where his book is heading is lying to you in a suave, writerly way.

I don't like lying, no matter how suave it is.

I'm going to tell you where my book is head-ing. That way, if you consider it [and me] despicable, you can leave us in the bookstore.

Researching the Angels

Until six or seven years ago I was certain that the Israelis were on the side of the Angels, *period*. No questions, no conditions, no mitigating factors—just the Good Guys versus the Bad Guys.

A few years ago I started doing some research. Research is pretty basic stuff: you follow clues, you go off in different directions, and you keep snooping until you find what you want. [It takes more stamina than brains.] The one thing you *cannot* do is have a closed mind. A researcher who has his mind made up in advance is *not* a researcher, he's an idealogue and a justifier.

[He's also a liar and a fake, but we won't mention that.]

The Vow

The first thing that strikes you [like an elbow in the groin?] when you begin researching the Arab/Israeli conflict is the unChristian feeling that everybody involved has taken a Vow of Closed-Minded Stupidity. The Arab/Israeli conflict makes smart people dumb, sensitive people brutal, and open-minded people pigheaded fanatics.

The Emperor's Privates

The second thing that strikes you is how dumb you've been. ['How could a smart cookie like me fall for **that** snowjob?'] If it was a good snowjob, maybe, but it's ridiculous!

It's like the Emperor's clothes: once you see the Emperor standing there with his little dingus hanging out, it's all you can do not to burst out laughing.

...to put it another way: I swear on everything I believe in—on my father's grave and my mother's laugh, on Caruso's voice and Malamud's "Jewbird" and Magic's no-look pass—*I swear to you*, I cannot see how any fair-minded person with an IQ over fifty can believe the Zionist/Jewish/Israeli version of what happened in the Middle East—*and* of what is happening now.

Mother Goose is more plausible than that!

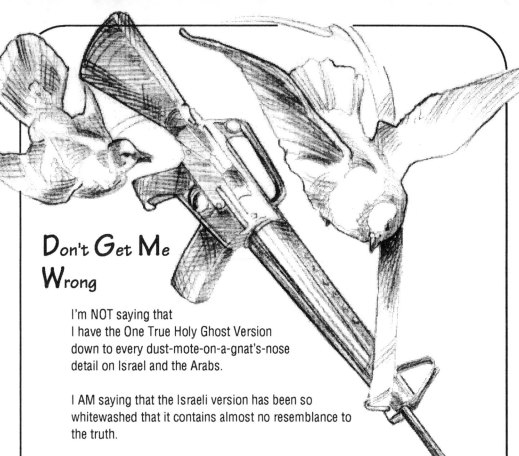

Don't Get Me Wrong

I'm NOT saying that
I have the One True Holy Ghost Version
down to every dust-mote-on-a-gnat's-nose
detail on Israel and the Arabs.

I AM saying that the Israeli version has been so
whitewashed that it contains almost no resemblance to
the truth.

I AM saying that the arguments for a Jewish state in Palestine were
[and are] so preposterous, so racist and so indifferent to the rights
and lives and religions of nonJews—and such a tricky insult to
democracy—that if they were made now you'd have no doubt that the
carpetbagger who made them was *at least* as crazy as Mussolini.

I am NOT saying that Jews should be expelled
from the Middle East.

I AM saying that the Palestinians, when **any
version** of the **real** story is told, have a case that
conforms to EVERY PRINCIPLE in which Americans and
others who pay lip-service to democracy believe.

That is what this book is about.

Read it with an open mind and decide for yourself.

Basic Questions

No Question is too Basic

I have a friend who specializes in asking mindbogglingly basic questions.

A few months ago he asked me a question so basic that it stalled my mind.

"I keep hearing about Palestine," he said, "but I can't find it on the map. Where in the hell **is** Palestine?"

My friend wasn't a scholar but he was smart and well-informed. If he didn't know the answer to a question **that** basic, maybe others didn't, so I began asking around. I couldn't believe it: most people didn't know the answers to basic questions, like:

- ◆ **Where exactly** *is* **Palestine?**
- ◆ **What exactly** *are* **Palestinians?**
- ◆ **Exactly what countries make up the Middle East?**
- ◆ **Are they** *all* **Arabs?**
- ◆ **Are they** *all* **opposed to Israel?**
- ◆ **Do the Arabs really "deny Israel's existence"?**
- ◆ **What does "denying Israel's existence"** *mean***?**
- ◆ **Why do Israelis say that there are no Palestinians?**
- ◆ **Is that denying the** *Palestinians'* **existence?**
- ◆ **Where did Palestinians come from?**
- ◆ **Who created Israel?**
- ◆ **Who owns the Occupied Territories?**

. . .and zillions of others, including *The Mother of All Questions*:

What in the hell are those Ayrabs & Jews fighting about?

QUESTION: Despite zillions of written & televised words on the Arab-Israeli conflict, people seem more confused than ever—or is that my imagination?

ANSWER: It's not your imagination. A poll taken during the Persian Gulf Crisis showed (I swear) that the MORE you watched TV, the LESS you knew about the Persian Gulf!

Q: But how is that possible?

A: It's the result of what professional bullslingers call 'Disinformation'. If they gave Oscars for Disinformation, the dudes who do the Arab-Israeli conflict would win every year.

Q: So, the more you learn, the less you know?

A: Right. And the more certain you become that your falsehoods are true.

Q: And the more intolerant you become of the truth...

A: ...and of the people who speak it.

Q: Where Exactly is the Middle East?

'Middle East' is a general area, not an exact place.

The countries that are *always* considered Middle Eastern are:

- Egypt
- Iran
- Iraq
- Israel
- Jordan
- Lebanon
- Palestine
- Syria

...and the eight countries of 'Arabia', the Arabian peninsula:

- Bahrain
- Kuwait,
- North Yemen
- Oman
- Quatar
- Saudi Arabia
- South Yemen
- United Arab Emirates

Countries that are sometimes considered Middle Eastern are:

- Cyprus
- Greece
- Libya
- Turkey

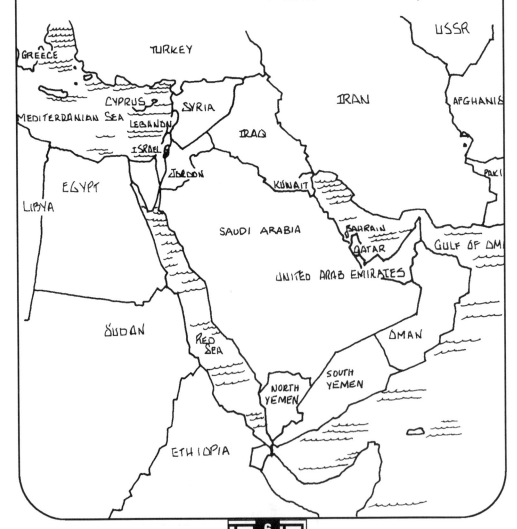

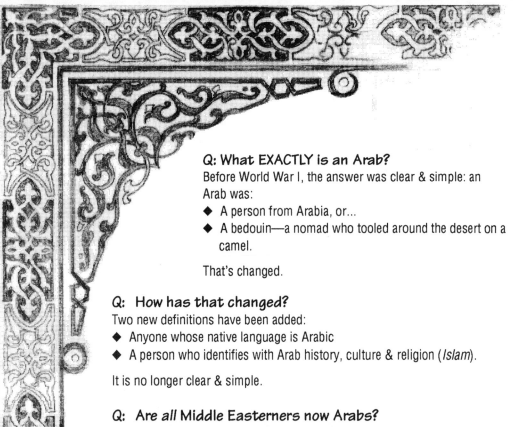

Q: What EXACTLY is an Arab?

Before World War I, the answer was clear & simple: an Arab was:

◆ A person from Arabia, or...
◆ A bedouin—a nomad who tooled around the desert on a camel.

That's changed.

Q: How has that changed?

Two new definitions have been added:

◆ Anyone whose native language is Arabic
◆ A person who identifies with Arab history, culture & religion (*Islam*).

It is no longer clear & simple.

Q: Are all Middle Easterners now Arabs?

No. There are still millions of people in the Middle East who are *not* considered Arabs—and millions *outside* who *are.*

◆ The eight countries of Arabia (listed on page 6) *are* Arabs.
◆ Iraq, Jordan, Lebanon, Syria, Egypt, Sudan, Libya, Algeria, Morocco & Tunisia are almost always considered Arab countries.

Turkey is usually considered Arab. Greece is *not* an Arab country.

Q: What about Iran?

Normal people consider Iran a *very* Arab country but experts don't (because most Iranians speak Persian, not Arabic).

Q: How many Arabs are there?

Somewhere between "more than 100 million" (*Compton's Encyclopedia*) and 260 million (as in "Israel is surrounded by 260 million Arabs"). Most scources are closer to the 260 million.

A F_{ew} H_{elpful} F_{acts}

- ◆ The 8 countries of the Arabian peninsula have a total population of only 30 million...so as many as 230 million Arabs live *outside* of Arabia.
- ◆ Islam: The largest unifying force among Arabs is the Islamic religion but:
- ◆ There are some 260 million Arabs.
- ◆ There are over 750 million Muslims (followers of Islam).
- ◆ ...so, even though most Arabs *are* Muslim, most Muslims are *not* Arabs

For a clear, concise description of Islam, see
Islam For Beginners by N.I. Matar.

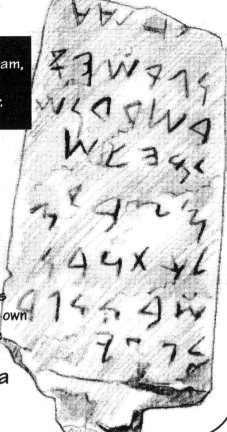

- ◆ Lebanon is interesting: it is (or *was*) primarily Christian & many of its natives spoke French & insisted that they were Phoenicians, not Arabs... yet Lebanon joined the Arab League.

THE LAST WORD... The semifamous General Rafael Eitan of Israel has his own sentimental definition of an Arab:

"The only good Arab is a dead Arab."

Q: What Are Arabs & Jews Fighting Over?

**Is there anything EXACT
or is the Arab/Israeli conflict
a beginningless,
endless,
ancient Middle Eastern feud
between the Hatfields & McCoys?**

Many 'experts' (geezers who write books with titles like *Understanding the Arab Mind*) talk about the Arab-Israeli conflict as if it were a feud between Yasir Hatfield & Yitzhak McCoy: ("There's no point in trying to make sense of the Arab-Israeli conflict. The violence between Arabs & Jews is part of an ongoing, centuries-old conflict...*et cetera.*")

That is a bunch of crap.

The Arab-Israeli conflict is **NOT** a "feud" between the Hatfields & McCoys. If any war is rational (and, if it is, we should redefine "rational"), the Arab-Israeli conflict is rational.

Indeed, the horror of the Arab-Israeli conflict is that it does make sense.

If they have any respect for logic, Arabs & Jews will go on killing each other for a long long time.

What are they fighting over?
What is *that* precious?   **Palestine.**

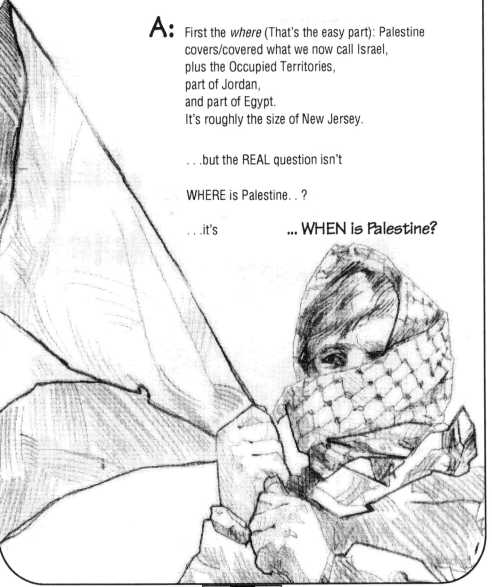

Q: **W**here is **P**alestine?

Why can't I find it on the map?

Why do Palestinians & Jews both say that it belongs to them?

Who was there first?

What is the historical background of the place?

A: First the *where* (That's the easy part): Palestine
covers/covered what we now call Israel,
plus the Occupied Territories,
part of Jordan,
and part of Egypt.
It's roughly the size of New Jersey.

. . .but the REAL question isn't

WHERE is Palestine. . ?

. . .it's   ... WHEN is Palestine?

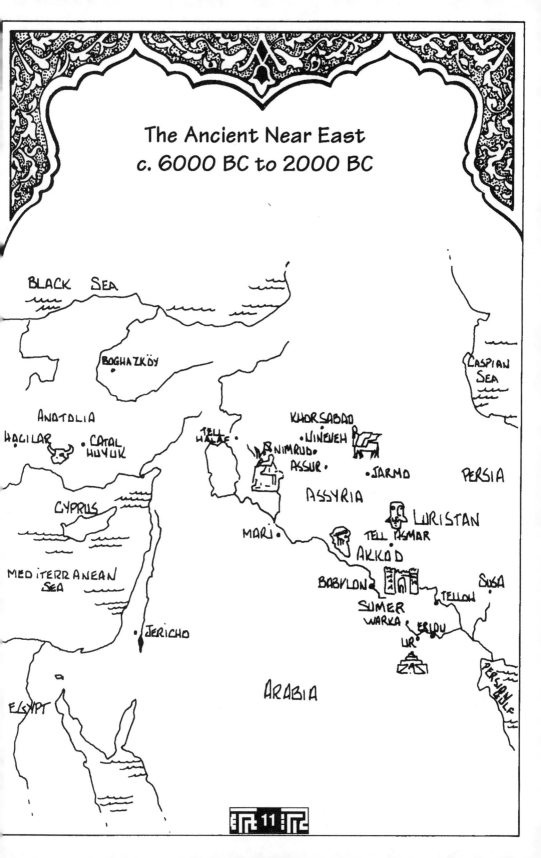

The Ancient Near East
c. 6000 BC to 2000 BC

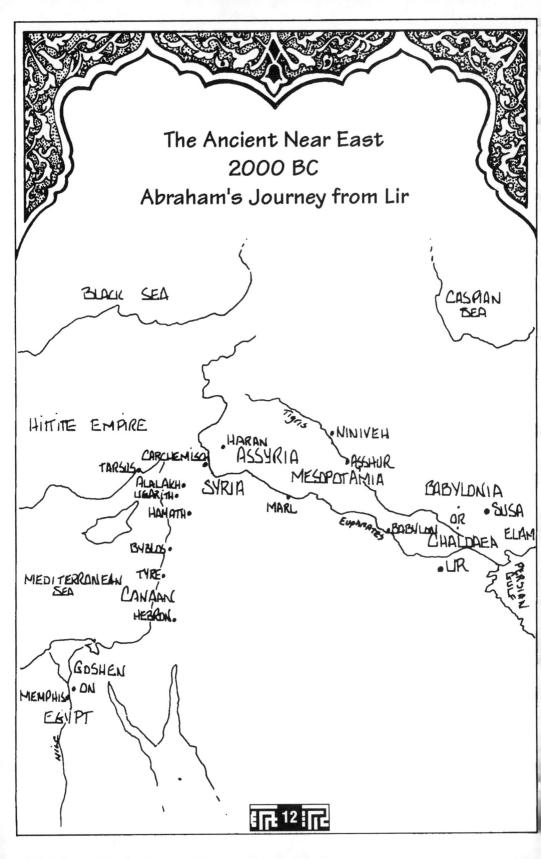

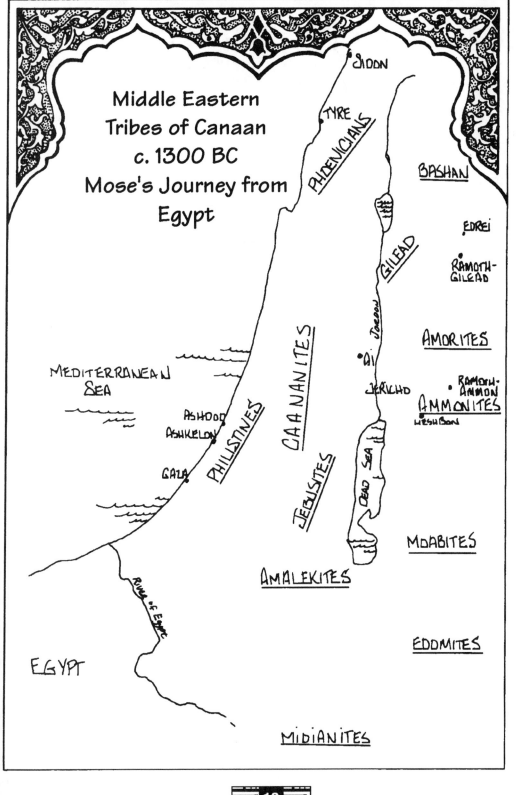

Middle Eastern Tribes of Canaan c. 1300 BC Mose's Journey from Egypt

SIDON

TYRE

PHOENICIANS

BASHAN

EDREI

RAMOTH-GILEAD

GILEAD

Jordan

AMORITES

MEDITERRANEAN SEA

Ai

JERICHO

RAMOTH-AMMON

CAANANITES

AMMONITES

ASHDOD

ASHKELON

PHILISTINES

HESHBON

GAZA

JEBUSITES

DEAD SEA

MOABITES

AMALEKITES

EDOMITES

River of Egypt

EGYPT

MIDIANITES

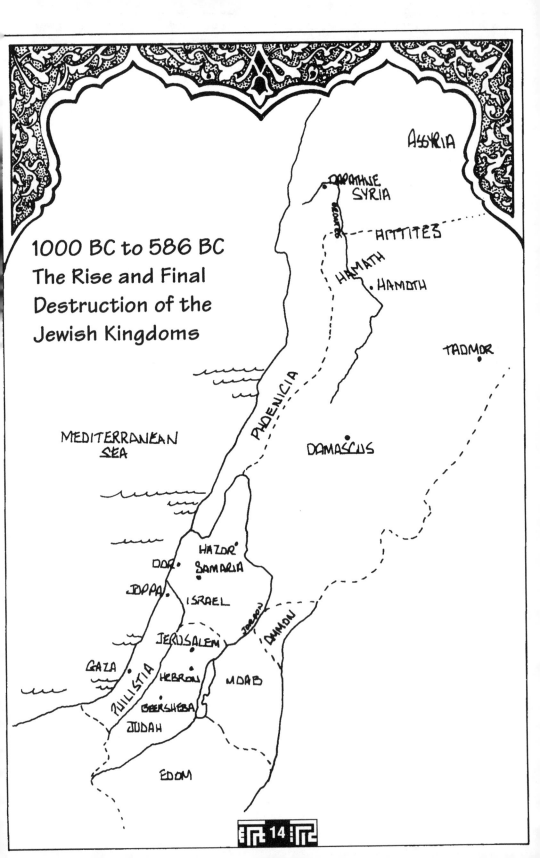

1000 BC to 586 BC
The Rise and Final
Destruction of the
Jewish Kingdoms

ASSYRIA

DAPHNE
SYRIA

HITTITES

HAMATH

HAMOTH

TADMOR

PHOENICIA

MEDITERRANEAN
SEA

DAMASCUS

HAZOR

DOR

SAMARIA

JOPPA

ISRAEL

JERUSALEM

GAZA

HEBRON

MOAB

PHILISTIA

BEERSHEBA

JUDAH

EDOM

PART
1

The MiddleEast in the Good Ol' Days

- ◆ Palestine BEFORE Ancient History
- ◆ Inventing Civilization—Ancient Cities of Mesopotamia
- ◆ Meanwhile, over in Egypt. . .

- ◆ Moses & Freud
- ◆ Ancient Israel—it's Birth & Destruction
- ◆ Greeks & Persians
- ◆ Alexander the Great & The Roman Empire

Palestine BEFORE Ancient History

"The greatest enemy
of knowledge is not
ignorance, it is the
<u>illusion</u> of knowledge."

Stephen Hawking,
prize-winning physicist.

If there's a way to say this without offending anybody, I can't think of it, so I'll just *say* it:

As a book of religion, the Old Testament is fine. As a highly mythologized history of Judaism's origin, the Old Testament is wonderful.

But as a history of the *non-Jewish* peoples of the ancient Middle East the Old Testament is like a 2000 year long Polish joke. ("Yo, Moses," Yaweh boomed. "How many Egyptians does it take to change a lightbulb?")

The Old Testament does a racist hatchet-job on some of the greatest, most influential civilizations the world has ever known.

As Jews know better than any people on earth, one man's holy book is another man's death sentence.

I'm sure that we can all benefit from knowing the truth about the Ancient Middle East.

The Neolithic ('New Stone') Age

Somewhere around 12,000 years ago, ancestors of what we now call Arabs began domesticating wild sheep, oxen and goats in the foothills of **Iraq**, **Iran**, & **Turkey**. While the men played with the animals, the women experimented with farming. This period of early farming is called the Neolithic Age (because all of their tools were made of stone and wood).

When people began settling down and domesticating animals, they also began to domesticate themselves. They began settling into villages. They learned that, instead of trying to grow and make everything yourself, it was easier to trade with someone else, so the villages expanded into trading centers.

The Ancient City of Jericho

About 10,000 years ago, ancestors of Arabs built the city of **Jericho**. Jericho is considered the first continuously inhabited city on earth. Archaeological evidence clearly shows that ancient people called the **Natufians** built solid, permanent houses, spread over ten acres. The Natufians irrigated and farmed the land and surrounded their ancient city with an elaborate defensive system.

That was 10,000 years ago. 8,000 years before **Christ**.
6,000 years before **Abraham**, the first Hebrew, walked the earth.

Jericho is located in what is now called the **West Bank**, part of the "**Occupied Territories**."

7000 BC

By then the Natufians had built a wall around the city of Jericho and constructed a 'road' that linked them with **Byblos** (located in what is now **Lebanon**). The Natufians made pottery & created artifacts from copper.

6000 BC

A charming but weird quote from Britannica: "The artistic achievements of this people are illustrated by some remarkable portrait heads, in which the features are molded over actual human skulls; these heads can probably be interpreted as evidence of a form of ancestor worship."

5000 BC

Britannica: "At this...stage...Palestine may have developed more rapidly than any other area in western Asia."

4000 BC

Another ancient people, the **Ghassulians**— probably from **Syria**—migrated into what the Encyclopedia refers to as "southern Palestine".

I nventing Civilization: Ancient Cities of Mesopotamia

The Sumerians:

◆ Invented the **Wheel**—the first wheels were potters' wheels

◆ Built cities—called **Kish, Lagash, Eridu,** & **Uruk.**

◆ Invented (pictograph) **Writing**—they wrote on clay tablets.

Sumer

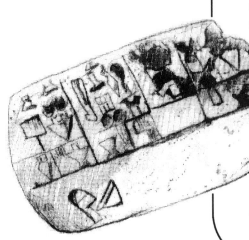

7,000 years ago, although stone-age farmers were building villages in Egypt and the Asian hillls, no one lived in **Mesopotamia** (now **Iraq**), the land between the Tigris and Euphrates rivers.

Around 4500 BC, chiefs began leading colonies out of the hills, settling on the fertile plains between the Tigris and Euphrates rivers, a land they called **Sumer**. The settlers drained the marshes and watered the desert, and within a short time Sumer bloomed.

In Sumer, around **3300 BC**, civilization began.

Sumerian merchants carried on a trade with people from India to Egypt. Sumerian temples ran the country. The priests invented writing and opened the world's first known schools to train scribes in proper Sumerian. The script, called cuneiform, was scratched on clay tablets, which have survived by the thousands to give us a record of Sumerian life.

Besides scribes, each temple employed carpenters, bricklayers, metalworkers, bakers, brewers (Sumerians liked beer!), butchers, potters, plowmen, shepherds, weavers, jewellers, hairdressers, and hookers.

The temples also sponsored festivals with music and sports.

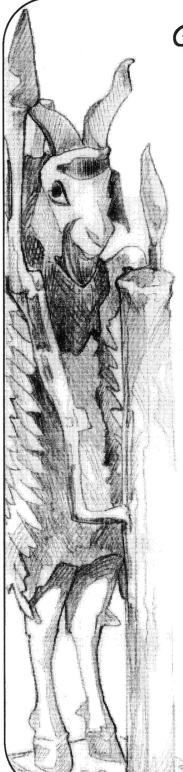

Gilgamesh

The Sumerians also wrote the first epic poem, **Gilgamesh**, about the exploits of **King Gilgamesh of Uruk**, the most famous hero of Sumer's Heroic Age (*c.* 2700 BC) who defied the gods, vanquished monsters, and turned down a roll in the hay with the Goddess of Sex and Violence!

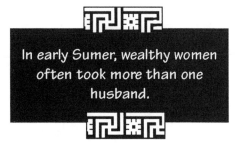

In early Sumer, wealthy women often took more than one husband.

Around 2500 BC the King of Lagash got his buns beat in a war over water. The King, who was not a good loser, tried to raise money for more war by taxing everything in sight!

The people of Lagash were apparently a lot smarter than us Americans. They threw out the old king and chose a new one, **Urukagina**, the first tax reformer known to history. Urukagina cut taxes, fired the collectors, and passed laws protecting widows, orphans and the poor.

Some things are just too good to last; a few years after Urukagina the tax reformer took office, King Zaggesi of Umma beat him up in a war. Urukagina, clearly another bad loser, put a curse on King Zaggesi.

(Stick around; the Fat Lady hasn't sung yet.)

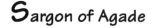

Sargon of Agade

Northwest of Sumer, between the city of Kish and the coast of **Canaan**, lived the **Semites**, a group of peoples who spoke languages related to modern Arabic and Hebrew. From the earliest days, Semites had also settled in Sumer and mingled freely with the Sumerians.

Semite (sem'it') n. One of a people of Caucasian stock comprising chiefly Jews & Arabs but in ancient times including Phoenicians, Assyrians, Babylonians & others of the eastern Mediterranean area.

Around 2370 BC, a young Semitic officer, **Sargon of Agade**, led a revolt that toppled the King of Kish. He smoked a few more cities before attacking Sumer. Sargon's butt kickin' army defeated the combined Sumerian forces—led by that dirty rat King Zaggesi. Zaggesi was marched to Kish in a dog collar!

Sargon's 54 year reign marked the first time in seven centuries that a non-Sumerian had ruled Sumer. By the time he died, the empire was in revolt but it didn't collapse completely until the time of his great-grandson, in about 2230 BC. After a period of anarchy, Sumerians reconquered Sumer and for 100 years their civilization flourished as never before.

The capital, **Ur**, grew huge on the wealth of the empire.

The Amorites

Then Sumer was invaded by a new tribe of Semites: not sophisticates like Sargon, but desert nomads (probably), the **Amorites**. The barbaric Amorites cut off the roads and waterways to the capital until the citizens began to starve. As the capital weakened, the **Elamites** (an old enemy), sacked the city of Ur [around 2000 BC]. . . then went home!

That was the end of Sumerian power. The Amorite savages took over.

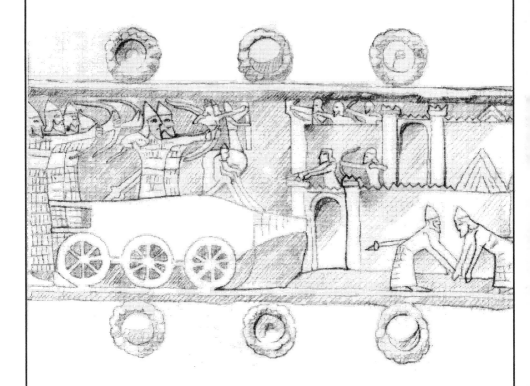

Like many previous barbarians, the Amorites grew civilized in Sumer. They liked Sumerian religion so much that they translated it into their own language (**Akkadian**) and began to believe that they themselves had invented it! Even then, Sumerian remained the "classical" temple language, long after anyone spoke it in the real world.

The Amorites spent a good deal of time fighting among themselves.

Hammurabi of Babylon

The Amorite feuding was stopped by the great general and statesman, **Hammurabi of Babylon**, whose reign began around **1790 BC**.

Hammurabi invented a legal code and made his God **Marduk**, king of all other gods. 'Ancient' myths were invented.

Hammurabi built his capital into the greatest city between Egypt and India, a center of art, science, and commerce. For the next thousand years, the land between the rivers was known as **Babylonia**...

Abraham   ...meanwhile, the city of Ur had been rebuilt and already one of its new citizens was itching to get out of town—an Amorite named **Abraham**. Abe's God had offered him a deal he couldn't refuse—"Go and I shall make you a great nation"—so Abe and his family left Ur. They raised sheep in the wilds of Canaan and passed the time by repeating stories they had picked up in Ur: "...and he built an ark forty cubits wide..."

After years of hanging out with his sheep Abraham noticed that, not only hadn't he "become a great nation", but he didn't have a single child. Finally, in his old age, Abe's wife **Sarah** had a son, **Isaac**. God told Abraham to sacrifice his son, so Abe—(a little too eager, if you ask me)—tied up his son and prepared to removeth his head. God let him off the hook at the last minute. Isaac taught his children to follow his father's God, and eventually Abraham's tribe became many tribes. During a severe drought, one of these, the tribe of **Israel**, pulled up stakes and moved on to the thriving river realm of **Egypt**.

Jewish myths claim that Arabs are descended from Jews (i.e., Arabs are descendants of Ishmael, Abraham's son by his Egyptian maid.) The real irony of that claim is that it's the other way around: Jews are descended from Arabs.
The logic is simple: Semites are either Arabs or Jews.
Abraham, the first Jew, lived (at the earliest) c.2000 BC.
Semites have been around since about 10,000 BC.
That leaves only two options:
◆ either Jews are descended from Arabs
◆ or a flying saucer dropped Abraham off in the middle of the desert around 2000 BC—

in the middle of a bunch of Arabs!!

Meanwhile, over in Egypt

Western historians have trouble with Egypt for two reasons: Egypt, the granddaddy of <u>Western</u> civilization, is actually in the Middle East. Africa, actually. Which brings us to the second reason: Westerners admit that the early giants of civilization were Egyptian, but they like to think that the Egyptians were White Guys with Rustoleum on their faces.

The fact is that many of the Egyptians we all know and love—including Nefertiti and Akhenaton, the pharaoh who probably invented monotheism—were black Africans. That fact is obvious in many portraits and steles, but it was missed by some archaeologists because, self-referring racists that they were, they didn't realize they were looking at black Africans. They thought they were looking at *deformed white people!*

Egypt's civilization was as ancient and advanced as Sumer's but life was easier. Every spring, the 750 mile long Nile River that runs through the desert of north Africa flooded just enough to deposit a fresh layer of rich soil over everything. Thanks to this fertilizing action, there was plenty for people to eat. As in Asia, when Egyptians began farming, populations grew and kings fought for control. For many years there were two kingdoms: Lower Egypt and Upper Egypt. Around 3000 BC, **King Menes** of Upper Egypt conquered Lower Egypt and the Dynastic Age began.

The easy life in Egypt gave its people a love of luxury foreign to their uptight Sumerian contemporaries. While the Sumerians were still wearing animal skins, the Egyptians had learned to weave sheer linen. Instead of writing on mud, they used a kind of soft paper made from the Papyrus reed. The elegance of their art was unmatched. Even their writing was beautiful.

The Egyptians even made an art out of dying.

In pre-Dynastic days, the king was put to death when he grew too old to rule. The priests comforted the old king with the thought that he would *live after death.* Eventually, the priests replaced the *real* murder with a *ritual* called the **Heb-sed**. When the king really died, they filled his grave with paintings and statues of servants instead of the real thing. As the kings grew rich, they commissioned lavish works of art...only to bury the masterpieces forever. (...or until some athiest tomb robber got hold of them.)

To protect the king and his treasure, they were sunk deeper into the earth, and the shaft was covered with a pile of stones, which was then covered by the "house".

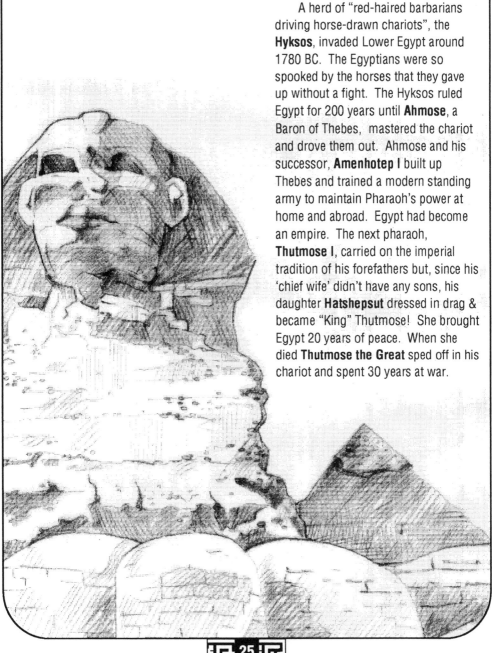

Around 2700 BC, king **Zoser** asked his architect, **Imhotep**, for a tomb that would display his unparalleled magnificence. Imhotep designed a tomb with one of the most complicated networks of underground tunnels ever built. He also turned the traditional tomb inside out: the old heap of stones came out of the "house" and became a 200-foot-tall pyramid.

Around 2550 BC, **King Khufu** decided to immortalize his name with a giant pyramid that took twenty years to build. We know him as **Cheops**, the Greek version of his name.

A herd of "red-haired barbarians driving horse-drawn chariots", the **Hyksos**, invaded Lower Egypt around 1780 BC. The Egyptians were so spooked by the horses that they gave up without a fight. The Hyksos ruled Egypt for 200 years until **Ahmose**, a Baron of Thebes, mastered the chariot and drove them out. Ahmose and his successor, **Amenhotep I** built up Thebes and trained a modern standing army to maintain Pharaoh's power at home and abroad. Egypt had become an empire. The next pharaoh, **Thutmose I,** carried on the imperial tradition of his forefathers but, since his 'chief wife' didn't have any sons, his daughter **Hatshepsut** dressed in drag & became "King" Thutmose! She brought Egypt 20 years of peace. When she died **Thutmose the Great** sped off in his chariot and spent 30 years at war.

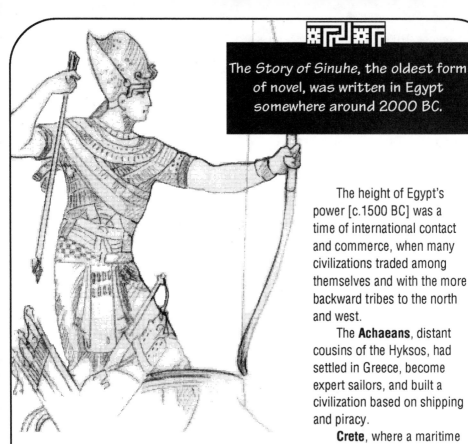

The *Story of Sinuhe*, the oldest form of novel, was written in Egypt somewhere around 2000 BC.

The height of Egypt's power [c.1500 BC] was a time of international contact and commerce, when many civilizations traded among themselves and with the more backward tribes to the north and west.

The **Achaeans**, distant cousins of the Hyksos, had settled in Greece, become expert sailors, and built a civilization based on shipping and piracy.

Crete, where a maritime culture had been thriving for a thousand years, was famous for its unfortified towns and topless gowns.

The original Hyksos migrated in all directions. Their language was the ancestor of the entire Indo-European family.

The **Hittites**, a charioteer elite, ruled Anatolia. They had found a method of smelting iron but were keeping it secret.

Bordering the Hittites was another kingdom ruled by a horsey set, the **Mitanni**, and downriver from them was Babylonia, still going strong.

Canaan, now ruled by Egypt, also bordered the Hittites, the Mitanni, and the sea. The **Canaanites** had so much business they had to invent the alphabet just to speed up their bookkeeping.

And to the East, charioteers called **Aryans** were in the process of destroying the ancient civilization of India.

Akhenaton

The Eyptian empire ran smoothly until about 1370 BC, when the new pharoah, **Amenhotep IV**, blew everyone's mind by announcing:

"There is *one* God."

Everyone knew that was preposterous—there were dozens of gods in Egypt alone!—but you don't argue with the pharaoh. (Especially when he's so far gone that he changes his name to **Akhenaton**, in honor of **Aton**, the one God.)

Akhenaton closed the old temples and had a new capital city built to honor the God. In their huge palace (its coronation hall was longer than a football field) the king and his queen **Nefertiti** devoted themselves to spiritual matters even though the provinces were in revolt. As the empire came unglued, so did Akhenaton. When he fell in love with his nephew, Nefertiti moved out.

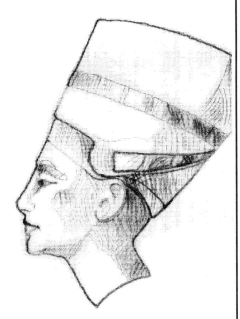

King Tut

When Akhenaton died, Nefertiti gave the crown to **TutAnkhaton**, a little boy. The famous boy-king became a pawn of the old farts, the old religion was restored. 'King Tut' died before his 20th birthday so his widow decided to marry a **Hittite** prince. . .

. . .but the young Hittite prince was murdered by Egyptians, so the Hittite King sent his army into **Canaan** (then part of the Egyptian empire).

Rameses the Great

For 60 years the Egyptians tried to expel them, then in 1290 BC, a cocky young pharaoh decided to finish off the Hittites for good. This king called himself **Ramses the Great**. In April, 1288 BC, four Egyptian divisions left Egypt, but after a month, Ramses the Great still hadn't found the Hittites. He needn't have worried; the Hittites found him, killed most of his men and took off. Ramses, still alive, hightailed it back to Egypt, where his greatness in battle was commemorated in song and stone.

The Hittites, meanwhile, took more territory and encouraged revolutions all along the Egyptian border. Ramses spent the next 15 years fighting to hold on to what he was already supposed to have. Finally he signed a treaty with the Hittites: he gave them the city of Kadesh and they gave him a Hittite princess. Ramses spent the rest of his 67-year reign littering Egypt with monuments to himself. (He would no doubt be honored by the fact that we named a condom after him.)

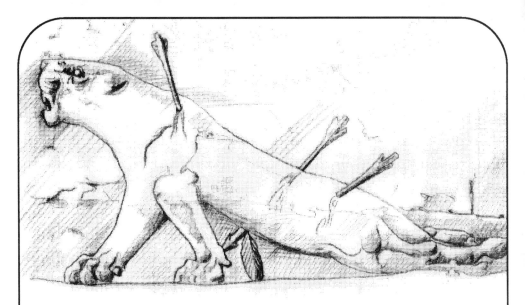

Egypt's Decline

1200 BC or so, began a dark age for the Mediterranean world.

With the death of Ramses in 1225, the pharaohs retreated from international politics. Within 300 years Egypt fell to foreign rule.

Beyond the Euphrates, the **Mitanni** were under attack by the **Assyrians**.

The **Hittite** empire, weakened by fighting with Egypt, collapsed within 50 years of the peace treaty, as hostile tribes attacked from all sides at once.

To the west, the **Greeks** were beseiging the city of **Troy** in a long war that would send refugees sailing all over the Mediterranean.

Canaan, too, was about to have its problems.

An army of slaves had escaped from Egypt.

4500 BC: Egyptian calendar, regulated by sun and moon, has 360 days, 12 months, 30 days each.
2772 BC: Egypt introduces a calendar of 365 days.

The Book of Genesis

Hebrew origins are lost in the misty past. Then Abraham, his wife Sarah, his nephew Lot, and their servants and flocks emerged from Ur in Sumer, heading for greener pastures in Canaan. Once they arrived, it's said, Abraham and Lot fathered many tribes. We'll skip the details and just mention that Abraham begat Isaac, Isaac begat Jacob—who changed his name to Israel after wrestling with an angel.

Jacob begat the twelve sons of Israel, one of whom, Joseph, ended up in Egypt with an Egyptian wife and a good job. During hard times in Canaan, Joseph offered his relatives some land in the Egyptian district of Goshen, and there they settled happily until, sometime after Joseph's death, they were enslaved.

So says the Book of Genesis.

There is no corroboration of any of that outside the Old Testament.

But it was a long time ago and most of the events were private.

Moses & Freud— the REAL history of the Old Testament

The Biblical Moses

Baby **Moses** was found in a basket floating down the Nile and raised among Egyptian royalty. When he grew up, Moses murdered a guy for abusing the slaves. He left town in a hurry and hid out in the Sinai with a fellow named Jethro who liked Moses so much he gave Moses his daughter Zipporah. Moses had a vision in which a Burning Bush told him to go back to Egypt and free the slaves. That made Moses so nervous that he made Zipporah circumcise their son.

When he got back to Egypt, he contacted Aaron and Miriam, the religious leaders of the Israelites. While Aaron and Miriam spread his message to the Israelites, Moses tried to cut a deal with Pharaoh. The slaves went on a looting spree, the pharaoh gave in, and a "mixed multitude", headed by Moses and Joseph's mummy, lit out into the night. The Pharaoh changed his mind, Moses parted the Red Sea, the Israelites got safely across but the Sea closed on the Egyptian soldiers who got what they deserved and drowned.

After the Israelites spent several years walking around the desert, tempers began to run short, so one wild and stormy day, Moses assembled the people before the Mountain of God. Moses wouldn't settle for any downstream laws, so he climbed straight up the mountain to get the laws direct from Yaweh—that was God's name before he turned Christian.

Moses was gone for a long time. By the time he got back down the mountain with the Commandments carved in stone, the Israelites were worshipping a golden calf. Moses, who had one hell of a temper, smashed the tablets, then ordered the slaughter of the calf-worshippers!

After the massacre, Moses climbed up for a fresh set of Commandments.

The First and most important Commandment was "No gods before Yaweh." The other commandments are the usual civilized rules against murder, theft and impertinence.

So—on to the Promised Land—**Canaan**.

Some spies were sent to check it out. . .

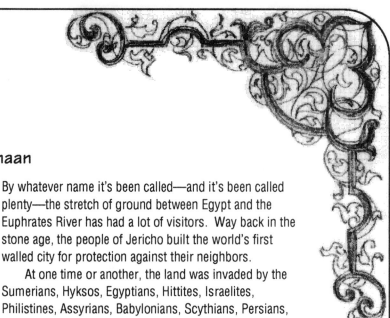

Canaan

By whatever name it's been called—and it's been called plenty—the stretch of ground between Egypt and the Euphrates River has had a lot of visitors. Way back in the stone age, the people of Jericho built the world's first walled city for protection against their neighbors.

At one time or another, the land was invaded by the Sumerians, Hyksos, Egyptians, Hittites, Israelites, Philistines, Assyrians, Babylonians, Scythians, Persians, Macedonians, Romans, Arabs, Crusaders, Turks, Englishmen, Zionists—but we're getting ahead of ourselves...

Then, as now, the country's landscape was unusually varied. On the coast were independent cities, centers of trade, and the source of the precious Purple Dye that gave the land one of its names, **Canaan**—"land of purple" in Ugaritic. Next comes the coastal plain, plowed by farmers and cut by gulches which carry the run-off from the mountains, where nomads and villagers coexisted. Further inland, the hills get wilder until they drop off to the deed, steep valley of the Jordan River, the Dead Sea, and the Oasis of Jericho, 1300 feet below sea level. Beyond Jordan, the land rises again, finally levelling off in the Arabian plateau.

It was a nice place when they weren't being invaded.

...when the spies returned from Canaan, their report was discouraging:

"It's full of people!"

The Israelites said, "The hell with it!"

So, Moses took them back to an oasis in the wilderness, where they stayed for 40 years, until most of the older generation, including Miriam and Aaron, had died. Meanwhile, the youngsters, led by Moses' protégé **Joshua**, began raiding some neighboring tribes and building alliances with others. By Moses' old age, they had become a fearsome army.

With Canaan in view across the Jordan, old man Moses went up for a few last curses..."A perverse and crooked generation...shall be burnt with hunger and devoured with burning heat...the sword without and terror within shall destroy the young man and the virgin, the suckling and the man with gray hair... I will make mine arrows drunk with blood and my sword shall devour flesh..."   (The guy was all personality.)

The Hebrews struck first at Jericho, then "put the Canaanites to the sword" and Canaanite culture to the torch while the Canaanites and Egyptians got the hell out of town as fast as they could.

The Israelites buried Joseph's mummy and took over the 'abandoned' land.

Of course, the Israelites didn't really kill ALL the natives, so they ended up living among surviving Canaanites, Jebusites, Horites, etc. which caused a certain amount of tension that may have had something to do with the fact that the Israelites rejected so many local institutions, like art, personal wealth, horses, chariots, fornication and anyone else's religion.

> ### The Song of Deborah
> During one of the Canaanite/Israelite conflicts the Canaanite chariots got stuck in the mud. As the Canaanite general Sisera, running for his life, passed a nomad's tent, a woman beckoned him inside. She gave Sisera some milk and set him at ease. Then she drove a tent peg through his head.
>
> This episode is rendered poetically in the *Song of Deborah*, thought to be the oldest passage in the Bible.

There's no saying how many heathens the Israelites would have exterminated if it hadn't been for some problems over in Greece...

Meanwhile over in Greece...

The Greeks shared in the general collapse of Mediterranean civilization that took place in the 1200's BC. Invaded from the north and hurt by a drop in trade, Greek shippers turned to piracy and war, climaxing with the 10-year Trojan War, which ruined most of Greece—and its neighbors. Whole tribes took to the sea, among them the **Philistines**.

During the reign of Ramses III, the Philistines attacked Egypt and were repulsed in a series of great sea battles. They rebounded to the coast of Canaan, every bit as desperate as the Israelites, but better equipped, with chariots and iron. Immediately they began to conquer the coastal plain, much to the alarm of the natives.

The first time that Israel fought the Philistines, Israel was roundly trounced.

The Israelites remained under Philistine rule for the next 20 years, until the emergence of Samuel, the last judge. The Israelite elders asked Samuel to appoint a King. Samuel saw big Saul walking along the road to Damascus.

A few weeks later Saul was appointed the first King of Israel.

A ncient Israel—Its Birth & Destruction

The United Kingdom
—1020BC to 922BC—

For his first act as king, Saul cut some oxen into little pieces and sent them throughout Israel with the message, "Whosoever cometh not forth after Saul and Samuel, the same shall be done to his oxen." They cameth forth.

Saul led the Israelites against a band of Ammonites. The Ammonites ran without a fight. Flushed with victory, he sent his son Jonathan to attack a Philistine garrison. In retaliation, the rest of the Philistines turned out in force. The Israelites ran for their lives!

As if things weren't bad enough, Samuel bitched him out.

Saul got so depressed that he raided the Amalekites for booty.

That was clearly against Yaweh's instructions: *kill everything that moves*.

To illustrate his point—something about Morality—Samuel took Agag, the captive Amalekite king, and "hewed him in pieces". Saul was so depressed that his friends hired a singer to cheer him up—a studly young guy named David.

The Philistines

The Philistines came out for battle. In the best Greek tradition, their huge hero, Goliath, paraded up and down between the lines with his shield-bearer. Israel's hugest was Saul, but he hung back. Instead, his singer volunteered. We all know how David faced Goliath without armor, how, using his deadly slingshot, he nailed Goliath smack between the eyes, how, as Goliath writhed in pain, David cut off Goliath's big Philistine head.

After the battle, Saul got a little jealous of David

So when the princess Michal asked to marry David, Saul, thinking he had David snookered, said, "She's yours—**IF** you bring me 100 foreskins of the Philistines." David did it.

(Can you imagine this kid out there circumcising the Philistines?)

One day Saul threw a javelin at David. David, beginning to feel that Saul didn't like him, went to the hills, where he was joined by family, friends, and the poor and oppressed. They became known as David's Mighty Men—especially the ferocious Joab, David's right-hand man.

The Mighty Men joined up with the Philistines and killed Saul. Then David led the Mighty Men to Hebron, where the tribe of Judah crowned him King. The rest of Israel followed **Ishbaal**, a son of Saul. Israel was divided for two years, until Ishbaal was assassinated in bed.

At about age 30, David became the **2nd King of Israel**. For his capital, David chose **Jerusalem**, a hill town occupied since 1800 BC by the **Jebusites**, a people Israel had never managed to conquer. David led an army against Jerusalem and took the city. Then he danced half-naked through the streets, singing hymns of victory. His wife, Michal got upset. He never touched her again. (He already had a couple extra wives.)

David & Bathsheba

One day David, while minding his own beeswax, spotted the bathing **Bathsheba**. Although she was married—to **Uriah the Hittite**, one of David's mighty men—David invited her in for a visit. He liked her so much that he had her husband killed.

After a proper period of mourning, David married Bathsheba.

They had a son named **Solomon**.

David spent his old age fighting to hold his kingdom together. Even the Philistines rose again. As David lay dying, his advisers tried to perk him up with the beauty Abishag, and his sons began eyeing the throne. One, Adonijah, staged his own coronation without inviting Solomon.

Solomon

After David died, Solomon murdered his brother and became the **3rd King of Israel**. Solomon became Israel's most powerful king: he laid heavy taxes, beefed up the chariotry, took hundreds of wives and worshipped alien gods. A few prophets denounced his rule but nothing came ot it.

Then there were Solomon's building projects. He made a deal with Hiram, king of the sophisticated seaport of Tyre. Solomon supplied gangs of laborers, 10,000 at a time, to cut Hiram's timber. Hiram supplied Tyrian ships, architects, engineers, metalworkers, ivory-carvers, etc. The result was a big palace for Solomon and a little temple for Yaweh.

In these splendid digs the conniving king lived out his reign in peace, receiving foreign dignitaries and dropping the little bits of down-home wisdom that made him famous.

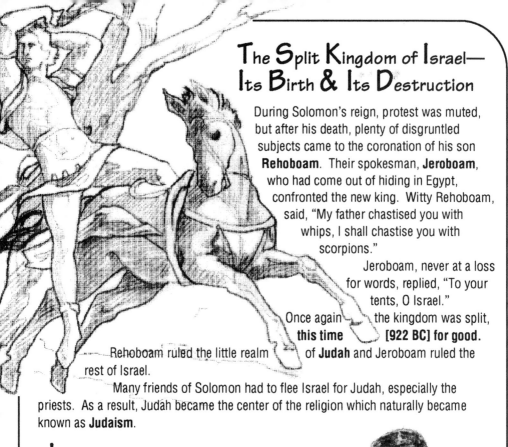

The Split Kingdom of Israel— Its Birth & Its Destruction

During Solomon's reign, protest was muted, but after his death, plenty of disgruntled subjects came to the coronation of his son **Rehoboam**. Their spokesman, **Jeroboam**, who had come out of hiding in Egypt, confronted the new king. Witty Rehoboam, said, "My father chastised you with whips, I shall chastise you with scorpions."

Jeroboam, never at a loss for words, replied, "To your tents, O Israel." Once again the kingdom was split, **this time [922 BC] for good.** Rehoboam ruled the little realm of **Judah** and Jeroboam ruled the rest of Israel.

Many friends of Solomon had to flee Israel for Judah, especially the priests. As a result, Judah became the center of the religion which naturally became known as **Judaism**.

Judah

Meanwhile, Egypt, which was making a comeback took advantage of the split to attack Judah, its neighbor. Rehoboam wisely submitted and pharaoh carried off Solomon's fabulous wealth.

Though poor, Judah did fairly well under Egypt's protection and the house of David ruled without interruption.

Israel

In Israel things went less smoothly.
After Jeroboam's death (c.915 BC), all his heirs were murdered by a rebel named Baasha.
Baasha's heirs were offed by Zimri, a captain of chariots.
Zimri reigned for one week before he was wasted by **Omri**.
Omri, who must have been a hell of a man, held on for life and left the throne to his son **Ahab**.

Assyria

Meanwhile, beyond the Euphrates River, from the hills north of Babylon, the kings of **Ashur** had begun the conquests that would build the **Assyrian Empire**.

The Assyrians inherited the religion, literature, and science of Sumer and Babylon—and added a few wacky ideas of their own. Like the Romans that would come later, the Assyrians were decent administrators and 'urban planners'—but where they really excelled was **war**.

With Assyria rising in the east, the kings of Judah, Israel, Damascus, Tyre, Moab, etc, suddenly put aside their differences. This coalition was able to hold off the Assyrians temporarily in a battle on the Karkar River, 853 BC. But the indirect cost to Israel was tremendous. 25 years earlier, **King Ahab** cemented one alliance by marrying **Jezebel**, a princess of **Tyre**. Now Jezebel was devoted to *her* god, **Baal of Tyre**. Ahab, an accommodating sort, built a temple to the god in **Samaria**, his capital. Baal and Jezebel were denounced by Israel's spectacularly intolerant prophet, **Elijah,** who had the priests of Baal *killed!*

Off with Their Heads

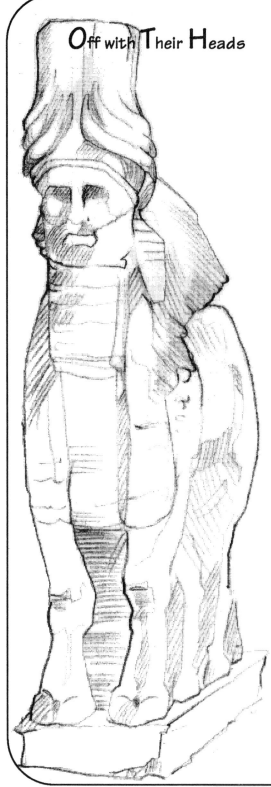

Fifteen years later: **Ahab** was dead; Ahab's son **Joram** ruled Israel and his grandson **Ahaziah** ruled Judah; **Jezebel** still lived; **Elijah** was dead but he had been replaced by the equally fanatical **Elisha** who had become the *leader of a large band of prophets*! **Elisha** decided the time had come for a final solution to the Baal problem...he sent one of his prophets to seek out **Jehu**, an especially nasty captain of chariots. The messenger found Jehu with some friends, pulled him into a house, anointed him king, and ran off. Jehu and his supporters drove to Jezreel, where King Ahazia was visiting King Joram.

King Joram said, "Is it peace, Jehu?"

Jehu replied, "What peace, so long as the whoredoms of thy mother Jezebel and her witchcrafts are so many?" Joram turned to flee and Jehu put an arrow through him. After Ahaziah, too, was cut down, Jehu rode into town to find Jezebel. He found Jebebel and his chariots trampled her body until nothing was left but the hands, feet, and head.

Then he wrote to the elders in charge of Ahab's 70 children, challenging them either to fight or to send in the royal heads. The elders didn't take long to decide.

The 70 heads were heaped in two piles at the city gate.

After disposing of the rest of Ahab's servants, priests, and courtiers, as well as 42 brothers of Ahaziah, Jehu turned his attention to Baal.

Jehu's Sacrifice to Baal

Jehu announced a great sacrifice to Baal—"Get your tickets, folks, you don't want to miss this!!!"
When the temple was packed full of Baal's priests, prophets, and worshippers, Jehu's soldiers barred the doors and slaughtered everyone inside. The statues of Baal were burned and the temple was knocked down and made into a public toilet.

History played a good joke on Jehu.
The only portrait we have of any Israelite king shows Jehu *bowing* to the Assyrian Shalmaneser III around 830 BC.

The Death of Ancient Israel

Israel eventually recovered from Jehu's coup and by 750 BC was almost having a golden age, then, about 740 BC, an Assyrian taxman was butchered by some citizens of Tyre. The Assyrian Army swept down, committed the usual atrocities, and tramped through northern Israel as a show of strength. By collecting an emergency tax of 50 shekls a head, **King Menahem** was able to buy them off for a time...but the sudden poverty sparked a revolt and the Assyrians came back to put it down.

Finally, in **722 BC, Samaria**, the capital fell.

The ancient kingdom of Israel was finished forever.

The End of Ancient Judah

In 701 BC, the Assyrians trashed part of Judah and besieged Jerusalem, but Judah survived for another hundred years.

It was the **Babylonians** who finally conquered Judah. In **597 BC**, the empire builder **Nebuchadrezzar** took Jerusalem and marched thousands of Jews into exile in Babylon. He returned in **586 BC** and set up a puppet prince, Zedekiah, to rule over those who remained.

It was another 70 years before the famous **Handwriting On The Wall** foretold the freedom of the captives.

Greeks & Persians

Some sources consider Greece part of the Middle East, most don't. I'm taking a 'functional' approach: I'll cover Greece only when it affects (or is affected by) Arabs and Israelis—and their ancestors. For the most part, that's the middle to late period of Ancient Greece.

The GREEKS—

Greece's Dark Age

Around 1200 BC, **Greece** was invaded by crude northerners called **Dorians**. The Dorian conquest sent Greeks scurrying all over the map. (That may have been where Israel's life-long buddies, the **Philistines**, originated.) Thanks to the Dorians, Greece entered a long **Dark Age** during which they became as dumb as everyone else.

> ...yes but, around 850 BC Homer wrote the Greek epics, Iliad & Odyssey.

As Greece emerged from the Dark Ages [around 700 BC], the **Spartans** (Dorian lords) were preparing to go to war and steal some land. Sparta was the meanest state in Greece. The prudent Greeks moved toward the sea, including the small islands off the coast.

Greece's Emergence

By 600 BC the coast of Greece was dotted with colonies and Greek trading boats were back in business. In the course of their travels, the Greeks saw once again what it meant to be civilized.

It made them unstoppable. They begged, borrowed and stole every idea from every civilized culture in the neighborhood, including the **Phoenician** alphabet and religion (the same Baal-worshipping, life-affirming, 'paganism' that sent the Israelites into a feeding frenzy) and Egyptian art, mysticism and "passion plays" in which the bloody parts were not real, they were *acted out*. The Greeks loved the idea, stole it, let it cook awhile. . .

The Glory of Greece

As trade (& slavery) increased many cities were overthrown by revolution. New rulers, dictators called **Tyrants**, put the slaves to work improving public places. Then the Tyrant Thrasybulos of Miletos hired a Philosopher!

The first 'professional thinker' was **Thales** (640-546 BC), a Phoenician. Thales predicted eclipses, figured out the height of the Great Pyramid by measuring its shadow and cornered the market in Olive Oil by making a small down payment on every olive press in Miletos! Thales' student **Anaximander** had the wild idea that the earth had evolved and that people were descended from fish. His smartass contemporary **Xenophanes**, said: "If animals, like men, could paint and make things, horses and oxen would fashion the gods in their own image."

And remember that simple Egyptian passion play that we left cooking in Greece's national psyche? In the 5th century BC, **Aeschylus, Sophocles**, and **Euripides** began writing full-blown **Greek tragedies** that we *still* watch to this day. Greece was going stark raving genius crazy. The entire country was exploding with brilliance in every direction. In the space of a couple hundred years the Greeks *invented* playwriting, democracy, philosophy and the Olympics; they revolutionized mathematics, sculpture, shipbuilding and medicine (not to mention the killing of philosophers).

I've barely touched the surface of what the Greeks accomplished. Greece reached a level of brilliance that no country has ever matched, but (as we'll soon see) every Big Daddy for centuries to come would try to **'Hellenize'** ('make Greek-like') his empire.

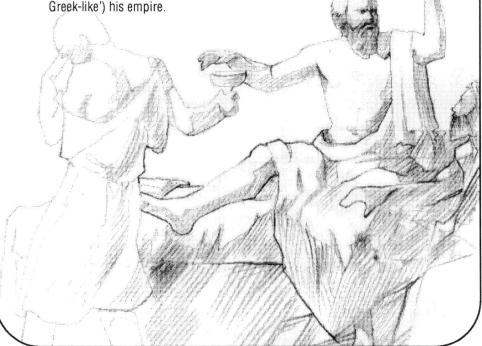

The PERSIANS—
the Achaemenid Dynasty, 550-330 BC

Around 550 BC, the Athenian **King Croesos** and his very large army went looking for the Persians. To his everlasting regret, he found them. King Croesos was set atop a pyre with several of his princes—then, at the last second, he was spared by **Shah Cyrus of Persia**.

The Persians' next target was **Nebuchadrezzar**'s rebuilt **Babylon**, the home of the exiled Israelites. Cyrus and the Persians took Babylon in one night. *Then Shah Cyrus allowed all captive peoples to go home and practice their own religions!* Some of them preferred to stay—the origin of Iraqui Jews.

Others returned to Jerusalem and [in 538 BC] began work on the **2nd Temple**. **Darius**, the new King of Persia, helped finance the building of the 2nd Temple. Despite the new beginning the Jews fought among themselves, neglected the land and let the walls of Jerusalem fall into disrepair.

50 years later, **Ezra** the Israelite scribe, "wept when he saw the lamentable state into which his religion had fallen." Ezra, like the other heroes of the Old Testament, didn't have a hell of a lot of religious tolerance—his first demand was that *"intermarriage with pagan women should cease."*

Thus Spake Zarathustra

Despite their religious intolerance, the Israelites borrowed freely from the religion of Persia. The Persians followed the religion of Zarathustra (6th cent. BC), who divided all things into Good and Evil.

Good was identified with the One God Ahura Mazda, creator of the universe, source of light and darkness, founder of the moral order, and judge of all being. An opposing force, Ahriman, was represented by darkness and disorder. All people were free to choose between Good and Evil, Light and Darkness, the Truth and the Lie.

During the **Achaen dynasty**, Persia [now **Iran**] ruled over different ethnic & religious groups from the Indus to the Nile. The Persian kings tolerated the diverse beliefs of their subjects as long as they obeyed the laws, paid taxes, and sent their sons to the Persian army. The Persian empire set the pattern followed by most of the multicultural dynastic states that have arisen since ancient times.

Especially that of Alexander of Macedonia—**Alexander the Great**.

lexander
the
Great

Alexander was born in **356 BC** in **Macedonia**, a kingdom north of Greece. Under his father, **Philip II**, Macedonia had become strong and united. Greece was reaching the end of its Golden Age. When Alexander was 13 years old, the Greek philosopher **Aristotle** came to Macedonia to tutor him.

Philip wanted to conquer Persia but he was murdered in 336 .

Two years later, in the spring of 334 BC, Alexander set out for Persia with 30,000 soldiers, 500 cavalry, plus geographers, botanists, historians, & surveyors. The maps they made were used for centuries. Alexander stopped by ancient **Troy** to pay homage to **Achilles** and other heroes of the **'Iliad'**.

Alexander's army encountered a huge force led by **Darius III of Persia** at Issus in October 333BC. After the Persian army fled, Alexander marched south along the coast of **Phoenicia** to prevent the Persian navy from landing. While he was in the neighborhood he also conquered Tyre and Jerusalem.

Late in 332 BC, Alexander reached Egypt. The Egyptians welcomed him as a deliverer from Persian misrule. He made sacrifices to Egyptian Gods and founded a new city on the Nile River, named **Alexandria**, after himself.

In the spring of 331 BC, Alexander again encountered & whipped Darius. **Babylon** welcomed him as a conquering hero and Alexander made sacrifices to the Babylonian God **Marduk**.

His men wanted to go home but Alexander wanted to press on to the eastern limit of the world. In the summer of 327 BC, he reached **India**, where he defeated **King Porus**, whose soldiers rode elephants. Alexander wanted to keep going but his soldiers refused—they'd marched 11,000 miles — so Alexander reluctantly turned back. The long marches & many wounds had so lowered his vitality that he was unable to recover from a fever.

Alexander the Great died in Babylon on June 13, 323 BC, at age 32.

The Hellenistic Age:

The three centuries after the death of Alexander are called the **Hellenistic Age**—the time when Greek culture spread through the Mediterranean. Through the influence of Alexander and his successors, the people of the Middle East adopted Greek dress, lifestyles, and culture and absorbed the vast amounts of knowledge found in Greek libraries that Alexander had placed at their disposal. Alexander began the fusion of Greek culture with Arab culture. Ideas & institutions of the Egyptians, Syrians, Mesopotamians, and Persians were absorbed into his far-flung, short-lived, realm.

Alexander's sudden death had left his generals without a plan for the areas they'd conquered. After 40 years of struggle and war, the **Ptolemies** controlled **Egypt** and the **Seleucids** ruled **Asia, Asia Minor,** & **Palestine**.

The Ptolemies became a province of the **Roman Empire in 30 BC**.

The Seleucid Empire continually lost territory until it was reduced to **Palestine, Syria, and Mesopotamia in 129 BC**. It continued to decline until it was **annexed by Rome in 64 BC**.

Rome, Rome, Rome, all you hear about is Rome.

The Punic Wars

When the ancient Greeks were reaching the height of their glory, the power of **Rome** was slowly rising. The genius of the Greeks lay in art, literature, science and philosophy. The Romans specialized in war.

After two centuries of war, Rome's only remaining rival in the western Mediterranean was the Phoenician colony of **Carthage**. Carthage was the big sea power, just as Rome was the land power. Carthaginian warships sank the trading vessels of any other city that tried to get a piece of the rich Mediterranean commerce. That didn't go over very well with the uppity Romans, so a fight for Mediterranean supremacy, the **Punic Wars**, began in 264 BC and continued until Carthage was destroyed in 146 BC.

The Roman Empire

Winning World Mastery

Rome was now well on its way to world domination. One conquest led to another. Italy, Sicily, Spain, Macedonia, Greece & Asia Minor were beaten and turned into Roman provinces. The new generation of power-obsessed Romans fought ruthlessly—and often ruined the countries they conquered.

The conquered lands were administered by greedy governors. The enormous taxes they extorted from the conquered peoples made the Roman governors rich and impoverished the conquered countries.

In Rome, the rich grew *so* rich and the poor *so* poor and numerous that the streets of the capital were flooded with desperate people who couldn't find work because they couldn't compete with the *slaves* who worked the great plantations. Two Roman noblemen, **Tiberius** and **Gaius Gracchi**, finally spoke out on the people's behalf. They proposed laws to redistribute the public lands and to limit the powers of the corrupt **Roman Senate**.

Both men were killed for their trouble.

The Empire is Established

The death of Tiberius [133 BC] marked the beginning of a century-long, multi-sided civil war that ended in the establishment of the **Roman Empire**. There was so much doublecrossing that, at one point Rome was invaded by a Roman army! The only thing that saved Rome from destroying itself was the emergence of **Julius Caesar** and his great-nephew **Augustus**.

It's a fascinating and, for democracy-lovers, a slightly scary story. Basically, Caesar saved Rome by 'disempowering' the Roman Senate and becoming Rome's dictator. Caesar was killed but the Roman Empire he helped build flourished, and Rome's provinces in the Mediterranean world came to resemble one huge nation.

"All roads led to Rome" . . .whether you wanted them to or not.

ROME—The End of Jewish Hope in the Middle East

Judah had been taken by the **Seleucids** [198 BC] without too much fuss but when the **Jewish Temple** was **destroyed** [**167 BC**], a Jewish priest named **Mattathias** started a rebellion. In 134 BC, **John Hyrcanus**, grandson of Mattathias, went a little crazy and razed the temple of the **Samaritans**, *a sect of Judaism.* As it is sometimes put, John Hyrcanus's "other" mistake was the forcible conversion of the **Idumeans** to Judaism. In 103 BC, a civil war broke out between different Jewish factions— the **Sadducees, Pharisees, & Essenes**. The Pharisees prevailed.

Most of what is commonly known of the Pharisees today comes from the New testament, in which they wrongly appear as villains. Jesus had been a Pharisee—a worker-rabbi—and his wrath had actually been directed against the priest class that the Sadducess represented.

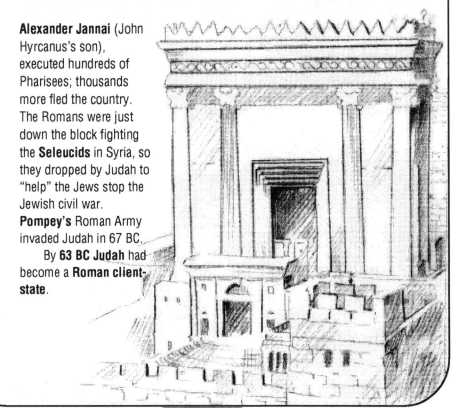

Alexander Jannai (John Hyrcanus's son), executed hundreds of Pharisees; thousands more fled the country. The Romans were just down the block fighting the **Seleucids** in Syria, so they dropped by Judah to "help" the Jews stop the Jewish civil war. **Pompey's** Roman Army invaded Judah in 67 BC.

By **63 BC Judah** had become a **Roman client-state**.

In **6 AD** the Romans made Judah a **Roman province**.

Jews had been moving out of the Middle East for hundreds of years but *that* was pretty much the last straw. There were a couple last gasps of Jewish revolt—**Masada** & **Bar Kokhba**—but the Jews & the ancient Middle East had had enough of each other.

A Summary of Jewish Countries in the Middle East

The united kingdom of Israel lasted for 98 years
—from 1020BC to 922BC—
In 922 there was a revolt and Israel split into two kingdoms:

Israel
The *northern* kingdom
lasted for 200 years.
—from 922BC to 722BC—

Judah
The *southern* kingdom
lasted for 336 years
—from 922BC to 586BC—

PART
2

1,900 Years of Jewish Absence from MidEast

- ◆From Christ to Constantine

- ◆From Mohammed to the Arab Empire

- ◆The Golden Age of Arab Civilization

- ◆The Crusades & the Mongols

- ◆The Jewish Diaspora—"In the Shadow of the Cross..."

- ◆The Ottoman Empire

From Christ to Constantine

At the beginning of the Common Era (A.D.—the time of Christ) the two powerhouses in the Middle East were the **Romans** and the **Persians**. **Palestine** and the rest of what we call the 'Holy Land' were part of 'Rome'.

(In those days, Rome was wherever the Romans said it was.)

In theory the **Roman Empire** tried to emulate the empire of Alexander the Great—unified, multicultural, tolerant, with free exchange of people, ideas, religions, and culture—especially *Greek* ideas and culture. (**Hellenizing**.)

In reality, the provinces were heavily taxed to support the huge Roman Army (which could be used against them at anytime). People moved to the big cities to find work but there *was* no work so they often became part of rootless mobs that rioted over social or religious issues. The poorer and more oppressed they were, the more they turned to religion but many had left their own countries, and their own gods (every country had its own god) and no matter how much you try to make somebody else's god yours, it isn't. Some tried the 'universal' religions of the Greeks but for most people those fancy religions pleased the mind but not the soul. Thousands of people with great expectations, no work, no money and no god—there *was* a god but he was a *small* god and he only worked in one or two towns. Can you blame them for wanting a big strong god, a god big enough to work in the whole world and strong enough to pull you out of that hole that Fate has put you in? Or at least give you hope. *If a man, through no fault of his own, has nothing in this life, will he never have another chance..?*

Jesus came along at a time when people needed a big strong God who was in charge of the whole world.

One of the great attractions of Christianity, especially to the thousands of poor, powerless and *future*less subjects of Rome (which was most of the Middle East) was the Christian promise of Joyous Eternal Life. The German philosopher Nietzsche (as he often did) went too far in the right direrction when he said that Christianity was a *slaves'* religion. It wasn't a slaves' religion, it was a *poor people's* religion—or a *regular person's* religion. All that stuff about rich men and camels passing through eyes of needles wasn't vague poetic buckshot, it was aimed directly at *poor people*. To people with no future on earth, Christianity offered Joyous Eternal Life. Sign here and you can have an After Life as glorious as a Pharaoh.

Christianity spread quickly throughout the Middle East during the first two centuries until the Romans decided it was a threat. It was officially banned by the Roman Empire. The Emperor **Diocletian** [284-305] tried his damnedest to extinguish it altogether but Christianity wouldn't go away.

What happened next is right out of Hollywood:

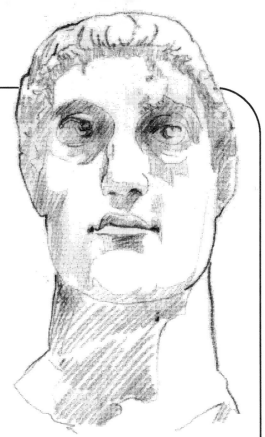

Constantine, the **Emperor of Rome**, decided to become a Christian!

That one event changed the course of history. If it weren't for Constantine's decision, Christianity might have disappeared like Zoroastrianism or Mithraism (or Communism)—instead, in one day Christianity went from a lunatic fringe religion to **The Official Religion of the Roman Empire**, the most powerful empire in the world. Constantine didn't do things halfway: in **330** he ordered the construction of a new capital which, naturally, he named after himself—he called it **Constantinople**. (...now it's Istanbul).

A Word About Persia...
The Roman Empire never monopolized the Middle East.
There was a state in Persia that covered Iran, Iraq, Afghanistan & Pakistan. Between the 3rd & 7th centuries, foreign scholars flocked to Persia because it was one of the few places in which they could teach and study unhindered by racial prejudice or religious dogma. Scholars driven from the Roman Empire (which turned even more repressive under Christianity), found refuge at the Persian academy of Jundishapur, which became a center for the preservation of the humanistic heritage of the entire ancient world.

Meanwhile, back in Rome...
Although the church covered the entire Roman Empire, the empire itself was divided into two parts in **395 AD**.

The **Western** half ruled from **Rome**.

The **Eastern** half [the **Byzantine Empire**] ruled from **Constantinople.**

The centuries after Constantine were filled with theological disputes that, to us, seem ridiculous, but which caused charges of heresy, dozens of different 'sects' and splits in the Church itself. The Roman church (headed by its bishop, the **Pope**) became dominant in Western Europe, while the church at Constantinople, (headed by its **patriarch**) dominated the East. Christians, from the pope to the paupers, fought over everything.

One Christian group, the **Arians** [4th century], taught that Christ, though divinely inspired and sired, was still a man not equivalent to God. At a church meeting in Nicaea in 325, Arianism was declared a heresy and it's followers were persecuted as if they'd been traitors to the Roman Empire!

Even for the poor and uneducated masses, the nature of Christ was a burning issue. While the scholars "disputed", *real* Christians brawled, rioted and generally raised hell over the true nature of the Prince of Peace!

A school of theologians called the Nestorians saw Christ as two distinct persons, divine and human but a Church council at Ephesus condemned them in 430 while the Monophysites, on the other hand, were certain that Christ had a single, wholly divine nature but the Orthodox bishops met at Chalcedon in 451 and declared the Monophysites heretics because the real truth, the Orthodox church declared, was that Christ was both perfect God and perfect man and that His two natures, though separate, were combined within the single person of Jesus Christ...

...can you imagine the collective sigh of relief that went up in the Middle East when Muhammad cut through all of that crap and said simply,

"There is no god but God."

"Many's the pregnant woman like you, aye and the nursing mother I've night-visited, and made her forget her amuleted one-year-old. Whenever he whimpered behind her, she turned to him with half her body, her other half unshifted under me."

by the 'wandering king', **Imru'al-Qays**

(Translated by some gent named Arberry)

From Muhammad to the Arab Empire

—but first a little background—

N₀ Place for Wimps

Except for the lush areas near the sea, **Arabia** (the Arabian peninsula), is a desert; even so, it has been inhabited for at least 10,000 years. To survive, people had to work together, so the desert nomads (**Bedouins**) organized into **clans** (family groups) and **tribes** (clans that joined) that migrated together and held their property in common. The men of the desert were feared & respected: any man who had the courage to cross the desert and appear at your tent was embraced as a brother for three days. On the fourth day, the brother better get his buns outta there.

The Warrior-Poets

The Bedouins, odd as it might seem, were obsessive poets. They loved poetry so much that they'd *stop wars and raids for a month* so they could recite their new poems to each other! By 500 AD Arabian poets gave public readings to enthusiastic audiences. Some of the best poets were authors of the *Mu'allaquat* (the Golden Odes), one of whom, the wandering king **Imru'al-Qays**, is quoted at the beginning of this chapter. It was written in the 6th century. (He may have been a dirty old man but that sucker could write!)

The Bedouin warrior-poets were such masters of the Arabic language & keepers of the ***muruwwah,*** that settled Arabs sent their children to live with the desert nomads to learn proper Arabic and to develop the manly virtues.

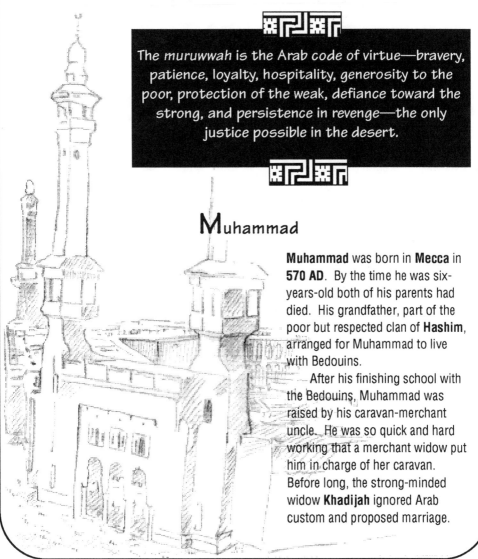

> The *muruwwah* is the Arab code of virtue—bravery, patience, loyalty, hospitality, generosity to the poor, protection of the weak, defiance toward the strong, and persistence in revenge—the only justice possible in the desert.

Muhammad

Muhammad was born in **Mecca** in **570 AD**. By the time he was six-years-old both of his parents had died. His grandfather, part of the poor but respected clan of **Hashim**, arranged for Muhammad to live with Bedouins.

After his finishing school with the Bedouins, Muhammad was raised by his caravan-merchant uncle. He was so quick and hard working that a merchant widow put him in charge of her caravan. Before long, the strong-minded widow **Khadijah** ignored Arab custom and proposed marriage.

When they married, Khadijah was 40 and Muhammad was 25, but that didn't stop them from having six children and a satisfying life.

Muhammad wasn't flashy. He was a hardworking businessman. The oddest thing about him may have been the fact that in 7th century Mecca, instead of taking a couple of young wives for sport, he committed himself solely to Khadijah, a woman 15 years older. (Prophet of God or not, you don't get *six* kids from a *spiritual* relationship.) Muhammad went on, straight as your Uncle Dudley, for the first forty years of his life.

Then, suddenly one evening, in the year **610**, all hell broke loose.

Muhammad was meditating in a cave near his house (maybe he *was slightly* unusual), when suddenly he heard the clanking of bells and a big voice ordering him to read aloud. Terrified Muhammad said "I can't read" and, fearing that he'd gone crazy, ran home to his wife.

Khadijah covered him with blankets and told him not to be frightened. She said that God had a mission for him. That frightened him even more. For the next 22 years until he died, Muhammad had—or thought he had—revelations from God. Those revelations, whether from God's mouth or Muhammad's mind, ultimately became the **Koran**.

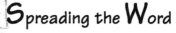

Spreading the Word

It was a full three years after that first episode before Muhammad began to speak out in public. He said that there was no unity among the Arab people—every man was out for himself and every tribe paid lip service to a different god—Arabs must unify, become one people with one God—the same God that Christians and Jews already believed in. Muhammad expressed his belief as plainly as possible: *"There is no God but God."* He called his religion **Islam**. It meant "surrender." Surrender to God.

The rich merchants of Mecca didn't like Muhammad. It wasn't his religion that annoyed them—they were businessmen: they'd worship Donald Duck if it didn't hurt business. What irked the fat cats of Mecca was the fact that Muhammad accused them of ignoring the *muruwwah*, especially the part about their responsibility to take care of the poor. At first they tried to buy Muhammad off; when he couldn't be bought, they started getting nasty.

In 616 the merchants boycotted the entire clan of Hashim, pressuring them to put a lid on Muhammad. The boycott lasted for three years.

In **619** Muhammad's wife **Khadijah died**; shortly after that, his uncle **Abu Talib**, the leader of the Hashimite clan, also died. Hashimite leadership passed to **Abu Lahab,** who quickly withdrew the protection of the clan. Without the protection of his clan, Muhammad was a sitting duck.

During the pilgrimage month in 620, Arabs from **Medina**, an oasis town 270 miles north of Mecca, told Muhammad that fighting between Medina's two Arab tribes had grown so bad they could no longer protect themselves against the three Jewish tribes with whom they shared the oasis. Because of Muhammad's reputation as an honest and wise man, they wanted him to come and arbitrate their quarrels. The next year the pilgrims from Medina needed Muhammad more than ever. In return for his services as an arbiter, they agreed to give sanctuary to the Meccan Muslims.

Muhammad knew that the Meccans were plotting to kill him. It was a good time to leave town.

The Hijrah

In **622** Muhammad and his followers left Mecca and went to Medina. Their departure, called the *Hijrah* (emigration), is considered the beginning of Islam and the start of the Muslim calendar. Muhammad got off to a great start in Medina by arbitrating the differences between the two Arab tribes. Muhammad wanted to unify *all* of the peoples of the Arabian peninsula, so instead of threatening the Jewish tribes, he offered to join forces with them since they were both believers in the 'one true God'. He emphasized the similarities between Islam and Judaism. He even observed the fast of **Yom Kippur** and led his people in prayer facing north toward Jerusalem.

They weren't impressed. How could this guy be a prophet, he wasn't even Jewish! As far as the Jews of Medina were concerned, Muhammad was just another dumb Arab. They told him to screw off.

Eventually Muslims changed the direction of prayer south toward Mecca and replaced the Yom Kippur fast with daytime fasting during the holy month of **Ramadan**. Islam was becoming more Arab.

Despite the fact that he was under constant attack from armies hired by the fat cats of Mecca, Muhammad preached compassion and justice.

Some days he lived up to it, some days he didn't.

The Massacre of the Beni Quraiza

Despite their religious differences, the Fat Jewish Cats of Medina had a lot in common with the Fat Arab Cats of Mecca—and Muhammad was a threat to both of them—so, more often than not, the Fat Jewish Cats of Medina helped the Meccans against Muhammad. (It wasn't personal; they'd have liked him just fine if he'd stayed in Mecca.)

Eventually, two of the Jewish tribes in Medina were expelled for conspiring with the enemy. They were the lucky ones. The third tribe, the **Beni Quraiza**, had not only refused to help the Muslims but sided with the Meccans in battles around Medina. The men were massacred and the women and children were sold into slavery.

The Conquest of Mecca

In **630** Muhammad marched on Mecca with an army of 10,000 men. He told his warriors beforehand that no homes were to be destroyed, and no women, children, or old people were to be hurt. Amazingly, the Muslims killed only a few people in their conquest of Mecca.

Bilal, a black Muslim soldier, climbed up the wall of the **Ka'bah** (one of the most sacred temples in Islam), sang out, "I testify that there is no god but God. I testify that Muhammad is the Prophet of God."

The Spread of Islam

Mohammed died two years later [June 8, 632], and was buried alongside the mosque in Medina. Islam not only survived his death but it spread with astonishing speed. Within 12 years, Islamic armies had taken Rome's Middle Eastern colonies (Palestine, Syria, Egypt) and beaten the Byzantines.

Barely a century after Mohammed's first terrified night in the cave, Muslims controlled an empire that stretched from Spain to the borders of China and the Arabs were entering a Golden Age.

"Regrettably, many Westerners still believe that the Arab conquest of the Middle East stifled its artistic, literary, and scientific creativity. On the contrary, it was the Arabs who saved many of the works of Plato, Aristotle, and other Greek thinkers for later transmission to the West. In fact, no area of intellectual endeavor was closed to Muslim Scholars."

from a Concise History of the Middle East, by **Arthur Goldschmidt, Jr.**

CHAPTER
13

The Golden Age of Arab Civilization

What do you DO with it?

After the Arab conquest of the ancient world in the 7th and 8th centuries, the Arabs had to answer the same question that all empire builders face:

You've conquered half of the world. Now what do you **DO** with it?

The usual answer is: you impose your culture—or lack of it—on the countries you've conquered. However. . .what the Arabs saw in the lands they conquered blew their minds. They'd never seen anything like it. They were fine warriors with a great army, but the culture of their desert home was simple and unsophisticated. Nothing in their culture could compare with the classical and Hellenistic heritage of the lands they overran.

They "sat as pupils at the feet of the people they subdued"—Phillip K. Hitti

The Arabs borrowed, imitated, *stole* every idea they came across—classical literature, Hellenistic thought, Byzantine institutions, Roman law, Syrian scholarship, Persian art. Before long they began using it creatively, combining it in different ways, creating new patterns. The result wasn't simply a mosaic of disparate cultures. It was a new creation with its own identity, infused with a new spirit and expressing a new order.

The great Arab cities—Cairo, Damascus, Baghdad, and Cordoba in Spain —became the intellectual centers of the world, producing the finest scientists and philosophers in the world. Arab doctors found answers to questions that Europe wouldn't even ask until the Renaissance. Arabs built the great mosque of Cordoba, devised algebra, and produced the first medical treatise on smallpox. While Europe wallowed in darkness and ignorance, the Arabs astonished the world with their architecture, mathematics, and medicine.

A Few Examples

◆ **Abu 'Uthman'Amr bin Bahr al-Jahiz** (776-869) brought Arabic prose to the heights of concision and clarity. **Al-Jahiz**, the grandson of a black slave, grew up in humble circumstances yet managed to get a broad education in his native **Basrah (Iraq)**. His wit and learning made him one of Baghdad's leading intellectuals. Of the more than 200 works that he composed, the most famous were his *Book of Elucidation and Exposition*, a study in rhetoric that covers history, natural science, and much more; and the *Book of Misers*, a witty and insightful study of human psychology. **Al-Jahiz**, who poked fun at himself as well as others—and even wrote essays on the relative merits of blacks and whites and the charms of slave girls—was one of the most versatile and stimulating writers in all of Arabic literature.

- **Avicenna** (Ibn Sina) (980-1037) Famous for his writings on medicine and psychology and his passions for travel, wine and women, Avicenna settled as a teacher in Teheran. He wrote a medical encyclopedia that was used as a textbook in European medical schools up to the 17th century.

- **Averroes** (b.1126) lived in Cordoba until he was exiled by the Caliph for not contenting himself with the true faith. He revered Aristotle, giving him the status of prophet, He believed, as did Aquinas later, that God's existence could be proved by reason alone.

In Medicine

- **Al-Razi** was the first to diagnose smallpox and measles and to use animal gut for sutures.
- **Ibn al-Nafis**, a Syrian, discovered the fundamental principles of pulmonary circulation.
- **Hunayn ibn Ishaq** (d.873) did his greatest work in the science of optics.

In Mathematics

Muhammad ib Musa al-Khwarizmi (9th century) produced a book on algebra which was in use in the West up to the 16th century.

- Muslims were using decimal fractions at least two centuries before Westerners knew about them.
- The Arab *sifr*, or zero, provided new solutions for complicated equations.

◆ **Abu al-'Ala' al-Ma'arri** (973-1057). Blinded by smallpox early in life, **al-Ma'arri** compensated by developing a stupendous memory. For those of us who buy the baloney that Islam is a dogmatic, intolerant religion, here are a few lines written by the Muslim **al-Ma'arri**, while living in the very Muslim city of Baghdad:

> Now this religion happens to prevail
> Until by that one it is overthrown,
> Because men dare not live with men alone,
> But always with another fairy-tale

This is syrupy but it expresses an attitude we pretend doesn't exist in Islam:

> Let all receive thy pity, none thy hate. . .
> For my religion's love, and love alone.

The Jewish Golden Age

One of the best things about the Arab Golden Age was that it nurtured—and was nurtured by—a Jewish Golden Age. One of the cultures the Arabs borrowed most heavily from was Jewish culture. Teaching the knowledge-hungry Muslims got the Jewish scholars' creative juices flowing. The result was a Jewish Golden Age, especially in Spain, during which doctors, poets, and scholars combined secular and religious knowledge in a way that has never been achieved since. The Golden Age of Arab civilization was influenced by Jews living throughout the Islamic world, especially in Spain. The great cities of southern Spain all had large Jewish populations.

A few illustrious Jewish dudes of the time:

◆ **Ibn Daud,** who in the mid-12th Century translated Hebrew, Greek and Arabic scientific and philosophical works into Latin.

◆ **Judah ben Samuel ha-Levi** (1075-1141) who was born in Toledo and studied at Lucena. His poetry in Arabic and Hebrew was very diverse and for the first time since the Song of Songs, introduced sexual themes in Hebrew.

◆ The most illustrious of all was **Maimonides** (b.1135-1204), a Spanish Jew who wrote in Arabic. He helped transmit Aristotle to the West. In Cairo he wrote his famous "Guide to Wanderers". Aimed at the poor souls who had lost their faith under the affliction of philosophy, the book argued that the pursuit of truth was religion itself. He invoked Aristotle as an authority on almost everything. These Arabic texts, quickly translated into Latin, had an enormous impact on the European clerical scholars. Maimonides was forced because of persecution by the fanatical Muslim Almohads, to escape from his native Cordoba to Cairo, where he combined Jewish scholarship with his work as court physician to **Saladin** (a famous Arab hero during the **Crusades**).

Thanks to the Golden Age of Arab civilization, a new energy would appear in the West to wake Europe out of the intellectual stagnation of the Dark Ages. . .but at what cost?

rusades & the Mongols

"God Wills It!"

Twenty years after the **Seljuk Turks** took Jerusalem, the *Byzantine* 'pope', for shifty reasons of his own, sent a plea for aid to the *Roman* Pope, claiming that the dirty rotten Turks were beating up and robbing all the Christian pilgrims who'd come to Jersualem to see God.

The Roman Pope **Urban II**, couldn't stand the Byzantine pope, didn't believe a word the Byzantine pope said, but for shifty reasons of *his* own, Pope Urban II, in 1095, gave a rousing speech urging all Christians to unite against the Islamic threat and save Jerusalem from "the wicked race" of **Saracens** (a fairly nasty term for Arabs & Muslims).

No speech in history has ever had greater results: fired up with religious zeal, clergy, knights, and real people shouted, *"God wills it"* and started packing their suitcases! Thousands left their homes in response to the papal call. Younger sons from large noble families, unable to inherit their fathers' lands, were especially eager to carve out new estates for themselves.

The First Crusade—from 1096 to 1099

On the way to the Holy Land the Crusaders killed thousands of Jewish 'infidels", especially in Spain.

In August 1096 the first real armies of knights and princes began their march to Jerusalem. Their famous leaders included Godfrey of Bouillon, Robert of Normandy, Raymond of Toulouse, and Bohemond the Norman. (One of the not-so-famous-famous leaders was a knight named **Walter the Penniless**!)

On the front of their tunics the crusaders wore a red cross.

(Those who returned from the crusade wore the cross on their backs.)

The Crusaders reached the walls of Jerusalem in 1099. They were so happy to be in the Holy Land that many of them fell on their knees, kissed the ground, and said with tearful gratitude, "Jerusalem, Jersulem!"

Only a thousand Fatimid troops guarded the city. After six weeks of fighting the 15,000 Crusaders finally managed to break through the walls.

On July 15, 1099, they entered Jerusalem, took the **Holy Sepulchre**, then robbed the nearby **Dome of the Rock**, the sacred place from which Muslims believe Muhammad ascended to heaven. Both Muslim and Christian accounts attest to the bloodbath that followed, as thousands of Muslims, Jews, and Arab Christians were beheaded, thrown from towers, tortured, or burned at the stake. A Latin chronicler of the time wrote: "The heaps of heads and hands could be seen through the streets and squares."

The Arabs were shocked.

They couldn't understand what they'd done to offend the Christians.

Second Crusade and the Fall of Jerusalem—1147-49

The renewed spread of Muslim power inspired the Second Crusade. Saint Bernard of Clairvaux preached it but refused to lead the expedition. Under Conrad III of Germany and Louis VII of France, it was so mismanaged that it accomplished nothing. A great failure, it returned in defeat.

In 1187 the famous Muslim ruler **Saladin** seized Jerusalem. Unlike the vengeful crusaders, he didn't slay his defeated foes. He let many go free.

Salah al-Din (1138-1198, known in the west as Saladin)
"Before I saw his face I was afraid of him, but now that I have seen him, I know that he will do me no harm" Those were the words of a Crusader, taken prisoner and brought before Salah al-Din, sultan of Egypt & Syria. The Crusaders found Saladin to be a noble enemy. Muslims loved him as a leader who united his people and turned back the tide of Christian invaders. Salah al-Din wanted to win back Jerusalem for Islam. He felt that it had been unfairly taken from his people by the Christian invaders. In 1187 he declared a "holy war". Gathering his forces from all parts of Egypt, Syria & Mesopotamia, he overran Palestine & captured Jerusalem [1187]. The one part he never did take was the narrow strip along the coast, part of Lebanon.

Saladin was always chivalrous and merciful. When his armies took Jerusalem, for example, he did not allow his soldiers to slaughter nonresisting civilians. Instead the captives were freed on payment of ransom. Many of those who were too poor to pay were also given their freedom.

After beating back the 3rd Crusade, Saladin signed a treaty in 1192, allowing Christians the right to visit the Holy Sepulcher in Jerusalem.

Both Muslim and Christian historians portray him as a paragon of bravery and chivalry—a perfect example of what the Arabs call *muruwwah*.

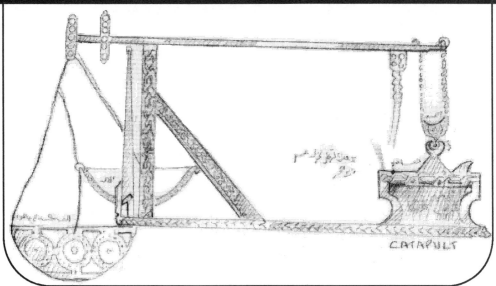

CATAPULT

Third Crusade a Treaty for Pilgrims—1189-91

Saladin's conquest inspired the Third Crusade. The leaders were **Richard the Lion-Hearted** of England, **Philip Augustus** of France, and the rickety old emperor of Germany, **Frederick Barbarossa**.

When they reached the Holy Land, Richard the Lion-Hearted and Philip of France joined the Christians besieging Acre. After a siege of 23 months, Acre fell in July 1191. Philip returned to France.

Richard stayed but couldn't capture Jerusalem from Saladin. However, he did get a three-year truce from Saladin in 1192. The truce permitted pilgrims to visit the Holy Sepulcher.

The Fourth Crusade—1202-04

The Fourth Crusade was meant to attack the Muslims in Egypt but the greedy Crusaders got sidetracked in Venice and helped the Venetians wipe out a few of their rival cities— *Christian* cities—including the great Christian capital of Constantinople!

The Tragic Children's Crusade

There were two Children's Crusades (1212) but I'll only talk about one. The **1st Children's Crusade** was led by **Stephen of France**, a 12 year-old shepherd boy. Stephen said that God had appeared to him in a vision on a hillside near Cloyes in France. God told him that only innocent children could drive the bad guys out of the Holy Land. King Philip of France refused to give his permission for a children's crusade and told Stephen to go home.

Stephen, under orders from God, ignored the King and kept preaching. His zeal attracted thousands of kids, most of them under 12 years old.

Stephen arrived in the port city of Marseilles with about 30,000 children. The ragged, half-starving youngsters waited there for God to part the waters of the Mediterranean Sea for their march to Jerusalem.

The slimy merchants finally loaded the exhausted little crusaders into old, rotted ships for "free transport to the Holy Land." Two of the ships sank, and all aboard drowned. The kids on the other ships were sold into slavery.

Later Crusades

The Fifth Crusade took place in Egypt (1218-21); by the time of the Sixth Crusade (1228-29), the Muslims were tired of fighting and conned the Christians into a little peace but in 1244 Turks seized the Holy City which led to the Seventh Crusade (1249) headed by Louis IX of France, who tried to take Egypt as the western key to Palestine, but Louis was captured and forced to pay a "king's ransom" after which he and Prince Eddie of England led the Eighth Crusade (1270). Louis, thank God,

A handful of Crusaders did stay. They built castles and created special orders of knighthood—the Knights Hospitalers & the Knights Templars. They swore up one side of Jerusalem and down the other that they'd stayed in Palestine "to protect the Holy Land" but they got so rich that Philip IV, the <u>King of France</u>, asked the Pope to help him confiscate some of their money!

died of plague, the crusade failed, and the Crusades finally ended.

By the close of the 13th century the Holy Crusading Christians had been thrown the hell out of the the Holy Land...wearing the blood-colored cross on their backs.

The Mongol Invasions—the Last Straw

The Arabs were still trying to repel the Crusaders, when they were visited by some guys who made the Crusaders look like Girl Scouts: **Genghis Kahn** and his **Mongols**. Genghis & Co. spent a few years [1218 to 1221] destroying cities in and around Turkey. The Mongols slaughtered 700,000 inhabitants of the city of Merv; they broke the dams near Gurganj to flood the city *after* it had been taken; they poured molten gold down the throat of a Muslim governor; they stacked the heads of Nishapur's men, women, and children in pyramids. The Mongols' record for mass murder and destruction stood unbroken until the time of Hitler and Stalin.

When Genghis Khan died in 1227 the Mongols decided to go kill everyone in China, Russia and Eastern Europe.

They didn't stay gone for long.

In 1256, **Hulegu** (Ghengis Khan's grandson) and the Mongols attacked Iraq. Some historians say Hulegu, who *hated Islam*, was "spurred into action" by the kings of Europe, who wanted him to help them kick some Muslim butt. (The Crusades were still going on and the Christians were getting smoked.) If he chose to exterminate the Muslims, Hulegu, *king of the Mongols,* didn't need help from those sissyfied Christians.

So Hulegu said "no thanks" to an alliance with Europe and, with encouragement from his wife—his *Christian* wife—Hulegu and the Mongol army crossed the Zagros Mountains into Iraq. The Iraqui Muslims resisted bravely but the Mongols flooded their camp, drowning thousands; then the Mongols bombarded Baghdad with heavy rocks flung from catapults until the Muslims surrendered [in 1258]. *After the Muslims surrendered*, the Mongols burned the schools and libraries, destroyed the mosques and palaces, and murdered a million Iraqui Muslims. The Mongols ended the party by wrapping all of the **Abbasids** (Iraq's royal family) in carpets and having them trampled to death beneath the Mongols' horses' hooves.

It was a lousy end to the prosperity and intellectual glory of Baghdad.

Everywhere you looked people were dying.

The Jewish Diaspora— "In the Shadow of the Cross..."

1100	1500 Jews flee from Germany
1228	Jews forced to wear distinctive badge in Spain
1266	Poland: Church decrees that Jews cannot live with Christians
1268	Total destruction of Jewish community in Italy
1279	Hungary: Church decrees Jews must wear red cloth on left side
1321	160 Jews buried in enclosed pit in France
1355	12,000 Jews massacred by the mob in Spain
1391	50,000 Jews killed on the Island of Majorca
1391	Jews massacred in Sicily
1399	First persecution of Jews in Poland
1412	Jews of Castile forced to live in separate quarters & wear badges
1420	Jews expelled from Lyon, France
1420	Jewish community annihilated in Toulouse, France
1474	Jews massacred in Sicily
1492	160,000 Jews expelled from Spain
1492	20,000 Jews die or are killed during expulsion from Spain
1492	Jews expelled from Sicily & Malta
1494	Jews restricted to certain area in Cracow—first Polish ghetto
1498	Not a Jew left in Portugal
1541	Jews expelled from Naples
1550	Jews expelled from Genoa

The Ottoman Empire

The Ottoman Turks

One of the dirty little ironies of war is that it matters less who wins the war than where it was fought. The Arabs had beaten both the Crusaders and the Mongols but after two hundred years of war in their own backyards, the Arabs were all used up. Everything was gone.

After the Crusaders and the Mongols had finished softening them up, the Arabs were easy meat for the **Ottoman Turks**. Since the Ottomans were Muslim and, for the most part, didn't displace the Arabs, losing to the Ottomans was less disruptive than beating the Crusaders and Mongols.

The Ottoman Empire was founded by a Turkish prince named **Osman** around 1300. The first period of Ottoman history [1300-1481] was one of continuous expansion. In 1444 the Ottoman Turks defeated a Crusader army and took Europe south of the Danube River.

The Crusaders lost all eight of the wars they started in the Middle East but the knowledge they got from the Arabs helped them break out of the brain-dead Middle Ages into the Renaissance—which would become the model for progressive Western civilization.

In 1453 Mehmet II did what so many Muslim rulers had tried—he attacked the walled city of Constantinople. But this time the Ottoman ships and guns succeeded where earlier Arab and Turkish attacks had failed. Constantinople was taken and and converted into the new Ottoman capital—Istanbul. Turks, Greeks, Armenians, and Jews moved into the newly opened city. Soon it grew as rich as it had ever been under the Byzantines. Christians and Jews were given religious freedom in the Ottoman Empire. This live-and-let-live policy was in striking contrast to the fanatical bigotry of Christian states at the time.

On the other hand: Mehmet II, clearly the mother of all control freaks, pioneered the practice of requiring all members of the government and army to accept the status of personal slave of the sultan.

Suleyman the Magnificent

The Ottomans defeated the Mamluks in 1517, which gave them control over Syria, Palestine, Egypt, and Algeria. As the new masters of the Middle East, the Ottomans ruled the heartland of Arab Islam, including Islam's holy cities, Mecca, Medina, and Jerusalem.

The reign of Suleyman the Magnificent (related on his mother's side to Marvellous Marvin Hagler) was a golden age of Ottoman power and grandeur. Suleyman conquered Hungary and Tripoli and extended his Magnificent empire southeastward through Mesopotamia to the Persian Gulf.

Sooley the Magnif, late in life fell under the influence of his favorite wife, who caused him to have one of his sons (by another wife) killed and another exiled, thus leaving the throne to her son, Selim II, also known (I swear to God—*all* of them) as "Selim the Drunkard".

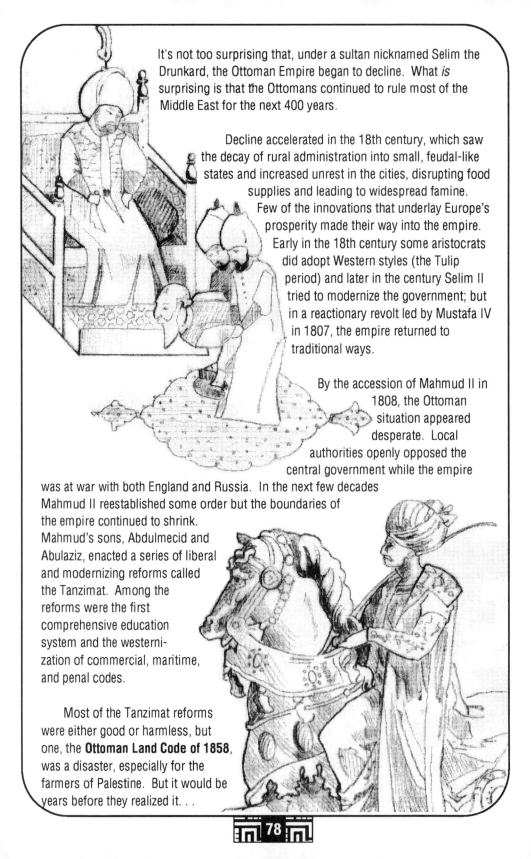

It's not too surprising that, under a sultan nicknamed Selim the Drunkard, the Ottoman Empire began to decline. What *is* surprising is that the Ottomans continued to rule most of the Middle East for the next 400 years.

Decline accelerated in the 18th century, which saw the decay of rural administration into small, feudal-like states and increased unrest in the cities, disrupting food supplies and leading to widespread famine. Few of the innovations that underlay Europe's prosperity made their way into the empire. Early in the 18th century some aristocrats did adopt Western styles (the Tulip period) and later in the century Selim II tried to modernize the government; but in a reactionary revolt led by Mustafa IV in 1807, the empire returned to traditional ways.

By the accession of Mahmud II in 1808, the Ottoman situation appeared desperate. Local authorities openly opposed the central government while the empire was at war with both England and Russia. In the next few decades Mahmud II reestablished some order but the boundaries of the empire continued to shrink. Mahmud's sons, Abdulmecid and Abulaziz, enacted a series of liberal and modernizing reforms called the Tanzimat. Among the reforms were the first comprehensive education system and the westernization of commercial, maritime, and penal codes.

Most of the Tanzimat reforms were either good or harmless, but one, the **Ottoman Land Code of 1858**, was a disaster, especially for the farmers of Palestine. But it would be years before they realized it. . .

STOP!

up to this point

What do both sides agree on?
Where do they disagree?

Is the disagreement critical, negotiable,

or mere smoke blowing?

◆ The Birth & Death of Israel/Judah are generally
agreed on ◆

◆There are disagreements over every detail of
everything else ◆

But the only thing that's important, damned near
everyone involved agrees on:

as of 1900

there is no Arab/Israeli
conflict

In fact,
Jews fared much better in
Arab and Muslim lands than in
European and Christian lands.

PART
3

The Seeds of Conflict

Palestine at the End of the Ottoman Empire

Nowadays most historians say, roughly, 'It is not really true, as most historians claim, that the 400 years under Ottoman rule was a Dark Age for the Arabs...'

Which means that, for the most part, it was. Things did start to perk up in the last half of the 19th century but the reality was that the Arabs had been swindled out of the Renaissance they'd been so instrumental in starting. The Renaissance had not only taken Europe out of the Dark Ages, but for 400 years, the West had used it as the foundation on which to build a new world with new rules: **Nationalism, Capitalism, & Democracy**.

The Arabs (better late than never) wanted some.

Under **Muhammad Ali**, Egypt had won its independence early in the 19th century and was on its way, culturally and economically.

In the 1870s and 1880s, the **Levant**—Syria/Lebanon/Palestine (Israel & Jordan hadn't been invented yet)—entered the world economy...and began inching their way toward Nationalism.

The Early Arab Quest for Democracy...& the Mandate

The American University of Beirut

In 1866, a Presbyterian missionary persuaded the American Board of Commission for Foreign Missions to build a university in Beirut.

In 1871, the Reverend Daniel Bliss announced, "This college is for all conditions and classes of men without regard to color, nationality, race, or religion. A man, white, black or yellow, Christian, Jew, Mohammedan, or heathen, may enter and enjoy all of the advantages of this institution. . . and go out believing in one God, in many Gods, or in no God."

That was the beginning of the American University of Beirut.

The American missionaries tried to convert Arabs to Protestantism by exposing them to the Arabic Bible; the unintended outcome was to make Muslim & Christian Arabs cherish their heritage of Arabic literature and history...*and* to have a say in controlling their own lives.

One of the first Arab nationalist parties was a secret society founded in 1875 by graduates of the American University of Beirut.

1876 Abdulhamid II, the Sultan of Turkey, agreed to the first constitution in any Islamic country.

At the same time, there was taking place a cultural, educational and linguistic revival throughout the Levant which was closely connected with the rise of **Arabism**, the precursor of Arab nationalism. The renaissance of the Arabic-language press was central to this revival and to the new thinking that came with it.

Two years later [1878], Abdulhamid II, <u>suspended</u> the constitution.

Although forced abroad by Abdulhamid's censorship in the years after 1878, journalism by writers from the Levant continued to flourish in Cairo. An ever-increasing number of Arabic newspapers, magazines and scientific journals were published in Egypt by Levantine authors, bringing to the Arab world the most advanced ideas of Europe and the first glimmerings of Egyptian and Arab nationalism.

The Young Turk Revolution—1908

People throughout the Ottoman empire couldn't help but notice that Abdulhamid was an incompetent, paranoid, dictator. A group of young dissidents decided to do something about it; they formed the Committee of Union & Progress, which became known as the **Young Turks**.

Their stated goals were:
- ◆ To strengthen the Empire, militarily & morally
- ◆ To give equal rights to all religious & ethnic groups
- ◆ To restore the Constitution
- ◆ And to get that meathead Abdulhamid out of power

Their victory was the first real breakthrough for Arab nationalism. It led to the restoration of the long-suspended Ottoman constitution. After 1908, Syria, Palestine, Lebanon and other regions of the Ottoman Empire made the transition from a regime of authoritarian despotism to one of parliamentary democracy. Suddenly, men living in Beirut and Damascus, Baghdad and Aleppo, Jericho and Jerusalem, were choosing their own representatives to an assembly in Istanbul.

Palestine at the End of the Ottoman Empire

In the year following the re-imposition of the Constitution, 35 new newspapers were founded in Greater Syria (another name for the Levant—i.e. Syria, Palestine & Lebanon). In **Palestine** alone, eight newspapers were established—the first two were ***Al-Quds*** in **Jerusalem** and ***AlAsma'i*** in **Jaffa**. 21 new periodicals prospered in Palestine between 1908 and 1914—plus dozens of other shorter-lived publications.

The number of schools (& the literacy rate) was steadily rising, partly because of the missionary schools: by 1914 there were almost 80,000 students in French and Russian schools in Syria and Palestine. The local governments also opened new, modern schools. A total of 221 state schools had been established by World War I in the Beirut/Northern Palestine area. According to 1914 Ottoman figures, in Palestine alone there were 98 state and 379 private Muslim schools.

OTTOMAN EMPIRE 1299-1918

MID EAST AFTER 1918

The Ballad of the Suez Canal

In 1854, **Muhammad Ali**'s son, **Sa'id,** granted a concession to a French businessman to build a canal across the Isthmus of Suez in Egypt. The British tried to block the project but once the **Suez Canal** was opened [in **1869**], England became its main user. Slippery old England managed to "buy" Egypt's control of its own canal.

In **1882**, Egypt's nationalist movement was growing so the British army went in to kill it. (If Egypt won its independence it might want control of its own canal!) The Brits left their army behind to "help" the Egyptians. The French wanted to help, too, but the British Army persuaded them to evaporate. As World War I approached, the Brits had over 100,000 soldiers in Egypt and they and the French were both wondering how they could get their greedy little hands on the Ottoman Empire.

World War I— The McMahon Correspondence: 1915-16

When the Ottoman Turks entered World War I on the side of the Germans, they unknowingly played right into the hands of England & France.

The British knew that the Arabs were fed up with being ruled by the Ottomans so, in **1915**, **Sir Henry McMahon** [British High Commissioner in Cairo] wrote to **Sharif Hussein** [Hashemite Arab leader] asking Hussein to start a revolt against Ottoman rule.

Hussein wrote back, asking for a pledge that Britain would support the revolt financially & politically; *Hussein made it clear that he wasn't going to revolt just to change masters—and* that he couldn't get the help of other Arab leaders without a British commitment that *all Arab lands under Ottoman control* would get their independence.

Hussein wrote several letters asking for clarification. (Apparently he'd dealt with the British before.) The letters they exchanged in **1915-16** (the "**Hussein-McMahon correspondence**") contained Britain's offer that if Hussein proclaimed an Arab revolution against the Ottomans, the British would help create independent Arab governments in Ottoman-held territory.

The Arab Revolt & the Mudros Armistice

On **June 5, 1916,** Hussein declared Arab independence & revolted against the Ottoman Turks. Arabs in Palestine & Syria joined the fight. The British sent in T.E. Lawrence—"**Lawrence of Arabia**"— to help the Arabs assist the Allies against the Ottoman Empire. Working with the British Army, the Arabs, led by Hussein and his sons **Abdallah** & **Feisal**, moved into **Palestine & Syria.** The Ottoman army withdrew and the Ottomans signed an armistice with the Allies on the island of Mudros.

At the signing of the **Mudros Armistice**, in **October, 1918**, the British & French again promised the Arabs the right of self-government.

The Arabs were excited.

PostWar Peace Agreements

During the war, **President Woodrow Wilson**, the foremost statesman of his time, had laid down the Fourteen Points upon which he wanted the Allies to build postwar peace. He denounced secret treaties, urged self-determination for all people, and proposed a "League of Nations" to head off future wars. When Wilson came to Paris to represent the U.S. at the Peace Conference, he was hailed as a savior.

The League of Nations was formed shortly after that.

In **1919**, **Article 22** of **The Covenant of the League of Nations** recognized the "provisional independence of the former Ottoman provinces."

Theodor Herzl & Early Zionism

Theodor Herzl was born in Budapest in 1860. He moved to Vienna at the age of eighteen and became an attorney. At the age of 31, separated from his wife and scarred by the suicide of his best friend, he left for France, where he was appointed correspondent for an Austrian newspaper.

Until then, Theodor Herzl, like most European Jewish intellectuals, believed that the solution to the Jewish problem lay in the assimilation of Jews into the countries in which they were living. The emancipation of the Jews and the recognition of their equal rights, initiated by the French Revolution, seemed to him an irreversible historical trend.

But the martyrdom of Captain Alfred Dreyfus—a French-Jewish career soldier who was unfairly convicted of treason in 1890s France (who *also* believed in assimilation)— and the wave of anti-Semitism that accompanied it, were to change Theodor Herzl's outlook entirely.

In **1896**, Herzl wrote & published **The Jewish State**, in which he argued that, for Jews, assimilation was impossible; the only real solution was a Jewish state—preferrably in Palestine.

For 2,000 years, when Jews spoke of "returning to Israel", it was only in a metaphorical sense—nobody ever took it literally. The idea of *literally* 'returning' to the Promised Land was not only politically questionable, it was also against Jewish doctrine. Religious Jews believed that they were not entitled to return to Israel until *after* God had sent the Messiah.

An organization of religious Jews, the *Neturei Karta*, who have roots in pre-Zionist Palestine, still believe that. They send out fliers with the heading: "WHY DO YOU VIOLATE GOD'S ORDER? IT WILL NOT SUCCEED."

Theodor Herzl was the most influential Zionist, but he wasn't the first.

Two of the first guys to disagree with God were (this shouldn't be a big surprise) Napoleon and the disgustingly rich Baron Rothschild.

An early Zionist book by the Russian **Leon Pinsker** (*Self-Determination*, 1882) was partly responsible for the **1st *Aliya***.

The 1st & 2nd Aliyas ("Ascent")

20,000 Jews moved to Palestine at the end of the 19th century. We call them the **1st *Aliya***, and we think of them as the first Zionists but their motives were purer than that: they wanted to get away from the Russian & Romanian pogroms.

After Theodor Herzl's 1896 publication of **The Jewish State,** the Zionists got serious. Herzl was made president of the Zionist World Congress, after which he went to the Sultan of Turkey and asked him for Palestine: no dice! Then he went to the British. They offered him *Uganda*!

The second large scale emigration of Jews to Palestine— the **2nd *Aliya***—followed Russia's abortive 1905 revolution. Most would have preferred America but the U.S. strictly limited Jewish immigrants. Palestine was the next choice, partly because Jews were treated better in Muslim countries than in Christian ones.

Not only that: Baron Rothschild, nice guy that he was, helped to send poor Jews on ahead to Palestine. He wasn't exactly doing it for *their* good. Baron Rothschild and the early Zionists *used* the poorest and most desperate Jews as their point men. Pit *poor* Jews against *poor* Arabs, so if the Arabs take exception to being run off their own land and things get physical. . .

The "idealists" could come along when it was a little safer.

Still, you have to wonder why they bothered. No matter what the Zionists wanted, the Palestinian Arabs had not only lived on the land for hundreds of years but they had a whole lazy-Susan full of commitments from the British guaranteeing that, at last, they would get their independence.

Why weren't the Zionists worried?

Did they know something that the rest of the world didn't?

Conflicting Promises, Expedient Deals, Rubber Documents ...& other Seeds of Conflict

A Sample of Rubber Promises to the Arabs

1915— We already mentioned the fact that Sir Henry MacMahon, British High Commissioner in Cairo, promised Arab independence to Hussein, Hashemite Arab leader, and their correspondence, **the Hussein-McMahon letters** ('Oh, you mean that Arab land!')

1915— There were other early deals between the Brits & the Arabs, including Sir Percy Cox's (British rep. in the Gulf) promise of Arab independence to Ibn Saud (Wahabite Arab leader).

1916— And there was the supernaturally underhanded Sykes-Picot Agreement in which France & Britain secretly agreed to give part of the Ottoman Empire to Russia, Greece, Italy, France & Britain. The Agreement clearly contradicted Britain's promise to Arabs. . but that was nothing compared to the Balfour Declaration.

The Balfour Declaration

Chaim Weizmann was a respected chemist, a British Jew, and a passionate Zionist who used his influence to persuade England's Lord Balfour to write the letter that became the "bedrock" of the Zionists' claim to Palestine.

The **1917 Balfour Declaration:** "His Majesty's Government view with favor the establishment in Palestine of a national home for the Jewish people...it being clearly understood that nothing shall be done that may prejudice the civil & religious rights of existing non-Jewish communities in Palestine".

There were people in England who weren't as dumb as Lord Balfour. Lord Curzon, Balfour's successor, saw through Chaim Weizmann's baloney:
"While Weizmann tells you one thing, and you are thinking in terms of a 'national Jewish homeland', he has something quite different in mind. He envisages a Jewish state, and a subject Arab population, governed by the Jews. He is trying to bring this about, screened and protected by the British guarantee."

And Don't Forget the...

1918—Mudros armistice: Ottoman Empire signs armistice & England & France once again promise Arabs control over their own land.

And the...

1918—Covenant of the League of Nations, Article 22: recognizing the "provisional independence of the former Ottoman provinces"

And Add a Couple of New Ones Like...

1920—The League of Nations made France the "mandatory" of Syria/ Lebanon; and England mandatory of Palestine/Jordan & Iraq. The mandatory didn't own the "mandate"; the mandatory was supposed to <u>teach</u> the mandate to govern itself like a democracy!
After all those promises of independence the British suddenly decide that the Arabs are too dumb to govern themselves!

1920-21—After anti-Zionist riots in Palestine result in the death of 51 Jews, the British, impressed by the Arab opposition, issue an official "White Paper", supporting Arabs more & Zionists less.

1923—After 3 years of Zionist pressure, the Balfour Declaration is written into the League of Nations Mandate.

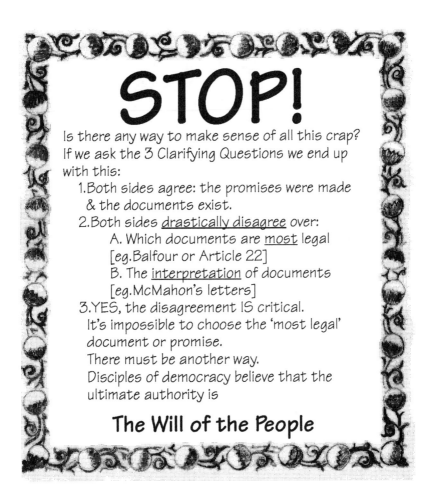

STOP!

Is there any way to make sense of all this crap?
If we ask the 3 Clarifying Questions we end up
with this:

1. Both sides agree: the promises were made
   & the documents exist.
2. Both sides <u>drastically disagree</u> over:
   A. Which documents are <u>most</u> legal
   [eg.Balfour or Article 22]
   B. The <u>interpretation</u> of documents
   [eg.McMahon's letters]
3. YES, the disagreement IS critical.
   It's impossible to choose the 'most legal'
   document or promise.
   There must be another way.
   Disciples of democracy believe that the
   ultimate authority is

The Will of the People

The Will of the People

The King-Crane Commission

When WW-I ended, no one could reconcile the claims of Arabs, Zionists, British & French so, in 1919, Woodrow Wilson and his democracy-mad Americans "dispatched the King-Crane Commission to the former Arab provinces of the Ottoman Empire to ascertain the wishes of their inhabitants regarding the postwar settlement of their territories." [Britannica]

The King-Crane report stated:

◆ 90% of Palestine's inhabitants were non-Jewish & did NOT want a Jewish state in Palestine;

◆ If they are given Palestine, "Zionists looked forward to a practically complete dispossession of the present non-Jewish inhabitants."

◆ The King-Crane Commission said that a Jewish state in Palestine would violate the Palestinian Arabs' right to self-determination; they recommended that Zionists respect the wishes of Palestine's inhabitants & find another place to plant the Jewish state.

The Zionists were furious!

(This is the part where I raise hell about highlighting the wrong events.)
The usual versions of Israel's history either don't mention The King-Crane Commission Report or they minimize its importance. In my opinion, any lover of Democracy must consider the King-Crane Commission's report a **major event**. The King-Crane report is definitive proof that:

◆ The Zionists knew they were acting *against the will of the people*.
◆ The Zionists knowingly subverted Democracy.
◆ The Government of the United States confirmed the legitimacy of the claim that Palestinians make today.

Some Quotes from the King-Crane Commission's Report

◆ "...a national home for the Jewish people is not equivalent to making Palestine into a Jewish State.."

◆ "...nor can the erection of such a Jewish State be accomplished without the gravest trespass upon the civil and religious rights of existing non-Jewish communities in Palestine."

◆ "In his address of July 4, 1918, President Wilson laid down the following principle as one of the four great 'ends for which the associated peoples of the world were fighting': 'The settlement of every question, whether of territory...or of political relationship upon the basis of the free acceptance of that settlement by the people immediately concerned, and not upon the basis of the material interest or advantage of any other nation or people which may desire a different settlement for their own exterior influence or mastery."

◆ "If that principle is to rule, and so the wishes of Palestine's population are to be decisive as to what is to be done to Palestine, then it is to be remembered that the non-Jewish population of Palestine—nearly nine-tenths of the whole—are emphatically against the entire Zionist program...   To subject a people so minded to unlimited Jewish immigration, and to steady financial and social pressure to surrender the land, would be a gross violation of the principles just quoted, and of the peoples' rights, though it kept within the forms of the law."

◆ "No British officer, consulted by the Commissioners, believed that the Zionist program could be carried out except by force of arms."

◆ "That of itself is evidence of a strong sense of injustice of the Zionist program."

◆ "The fact came out repeatedly in the Commission's conference with Jewish representatives that the Zionists looked forward to a pract*cally complete dispossession* of the present non-Jewish inhabitants of Palestine."

◆ **"the initial claim, often submitted by Zionist representatives, that they have a 'right' to Palestine, based on an occupation of two thousand years ago, can hardly be seriously considered."**

Which leaves us with two very perplexing questions:

Q: Why did the "great western democracies" support a travesty in which the will of 10% of the people overruled the other 90%?

Q: How did Jews, usually among the most morally sensitive people on earth, justify taking a country in which Jews had not lived for 2000 years?

A Country Without People

"A country without a people for a people without a country."

Chaim Weizman, President of the World Zionist Congress

Back to Theodor Herzl's Famous Book

Four hypotheses were at the basis of Herzl's idea of Zionism:

1. The existence of a Jewish people
2. The impossibility of assimilation into the societies in which Jews live
3. The Jewish people's right to the Promised Land
4. The non-existence in this [Promised] land of another people, who also had rights.

You don't have to be Einstein to notice that Number Four might turn out to be just a little bit of a problem. Zionists knew from day one that the weakest link in their plan to turn Palestine into Israel was tapdancing around the fact that Palestine was already someone else's homeland.

It'd be a piece of cake to sell Jews—especially the poorest and most oppressed ones—the romantic, mystical, heroic notion of returning to Biblical Israel—*if only* those damned Palestinians weren't there. The Zionists knew what would happen if they admitted the truth!

(This is the reality, dudes: Palestine is full. There are people all over Palestine and they've lived there for hundreds, maybe thousands, of years. They aren't really modern yet but they've made a good start. They have decent schools, they put out their own newspapers, they write poetry. The women are beautiful, the men are circumcised, and all the decent land is already being farmed. So whaddya say we go throw the suckers out!)

The Jewish people weren't ghouls. Jews were as humane as any people on earth. They would never try to take over a country that was full of people—especially people who'd lived there for centuries...people who'd never done anything to them. (At least most Jews wouldn't.)

(I hope they wouldn't.)

So what did the Zionists do? In the words of Professor John Ruedy, "it was convenient for Zionists and their supporters to picture Palestine as a wasteland before they came." At a 1914 Zionist meeting in Paris, Chaim Weizman came up with that catchy slogan: "A country without a people for a people without a country." It became the heart of an intentionally misleading advertising campaign to "sell" diaspora Jews on the idea of moving to Palestine.

The early Zionists did such a good job of snow jobbing the general public that Jews who went to Palestine were often shocked to see that people actually lived there.

After visiting Palestine for the first time, the famous Jewish author, Ahad Ha'am (Asher Ginsberg), wrote in 1891: "We abroad are used to believing that Eretz Israel is now almost totally desolate, a desert that is not sowed, and that anyone who wishes to purchase land there may come and purchase as much as he desires. But in truth this is not the case. Throughout the country it is difficult to find fields that are not sowed. Only sand dunes and stony mountains that are not fit to grow anything but fruit trees—and this only after hard labor and great expense of clearing and reclamation—only these are not cultivated."

He also said that the Zionists "treat the Arabs with hostility and cruelty, deprive them of their rights, offend them without cause, and even boast of these deeds." He was so disgusted with Zionism that he said, "If this is the 'Messiah', then I do not wish to see his coming."

They say that when Max Nordau, Theodor Herzl's second banana, learned that there were Palestinian Arabs living in Palestine, he said to Herzl, **"I never realized this—we are committing an injustice."**

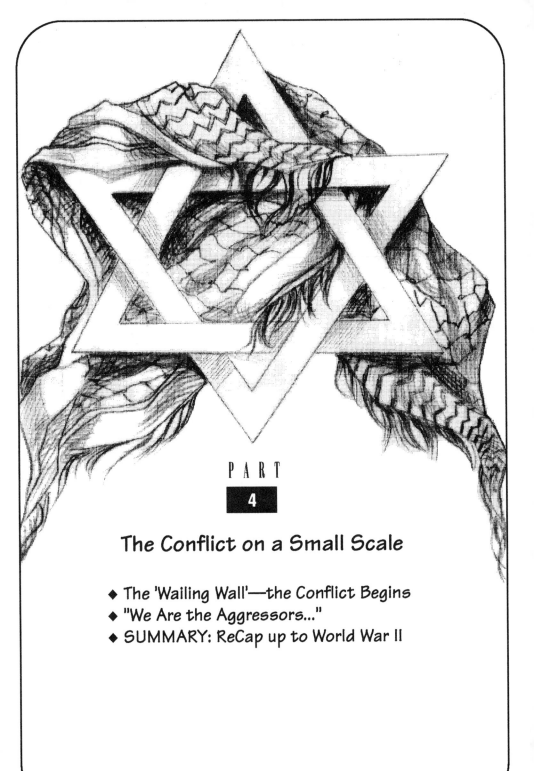

The Conflict on a Small Scale

- ◆ The 'Wailing Wall'—the Conflict Begins
- ◆ "We Are the Aggressors..."
- ◆ SUMMARY: ReCap up to World War II

Withdraw thy foot from thy neighbor's house, lest he be weary of thee, and so hate thee.

Proverbs, 25:17

The Conflict Between Arabs & Jews Begins

From the early stages of Zionist colonization, Palestinian farmers were run off of land they'd 'owned' for centuries. At the exact time when Palestinians and other Arabs were moving toward nationalism and self-determination, the Ottoman Turks were secretly selling Palestinian land to Zionist colonists. Worst of all, the Palestinians didn't know that they'd ceased to be the legal owners until Jewish settlers told them that the Jewish Agency had bought the land from absentee landlords—thanks to the 1858 Ottoman Land Code.

The Ottoman Land Code of 1858

Although it became official in 1858, the Ottoman Land Code was put into effect in Syria and Palestine over a period of decades, one sneaky little inch at a time. The Land Code required the registration of farm land, most of which had never before been registered and which had been treated according to traditional forms of land tenure—*masha'a*, communal usufruct.

("**Usufruct**" is the legal right to use, profit and benefit from something you don't own.)

The new law meant that for the first time a peasant could be deprived of the right to live on and cultivate "his" land and pass it on to his heirs—a right that had formerly been considered "unalienable."

Under the 1858 law, if peasants with long-standing rights failed to register—which they often did—rich guys who were good at manipulating the law registered large areas of land as theirs—and then sold it to the Jewish Agency, who was more than happy with the slippery arrangement.

Predictably, the expulsion of Palestinian farmers by the new Jewish settlers frequently led to confrontations with the local populace. The early attempt of the Jewish Colonization Association [JCA] to "remove the peasants who cultivated the land" from a large piece of land in the Tiberias district met with stiff resistance from the Arab villagers of al-Shajara, Misha, and Melhamiyya. According to the account of the incident by H.M. Kalvariski, an official of the JCA, the peasants not only refused to move off their land but they shot at the guy who engineered the deal; Ottoman troops were brought in and many tenants were arrested and taken to prison.

This so offended the Arab nationalists that the Arab district officer of Tiberias, **Amir Amin Arslan**, opposed the transaction on nationalist grounds. He was overruled by his Turkish superiors but even so he continued to "resist the de-Arabization of the district".

After the re-imposition of the Ottoman Constitution, which guaranteed free speech and provided for the election of a parliament, Amir Amin Arslan won an election and represented Arab provinces in the Ottoman Parliament.

A little before World War I, serious disputes arose over land ownership so the secret Jewish army, *Hashomer,* went public.

Throughout Palestine, Arab district officers supported Palestinian farmers threatened with dispossession and tried to resist their Turkish bosses.

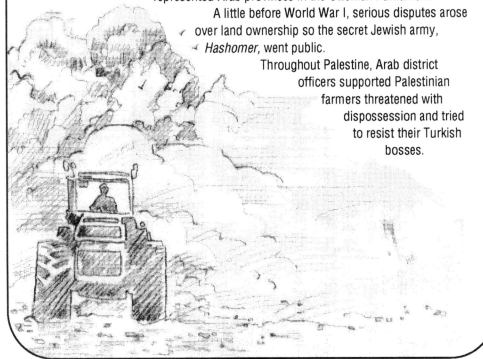

Shukri al-'Asali (aka, 'Saladin')

One district officer who became famous in the **"Afula affair"** was **Shukri al-'Asali**, the governor of Nazareth. al-'Asali was a member of a prominent Damascus family who had been educated at Mulkiya College in Istanbul, after which he had held a number of government posts. He outright refused to throw the Palestinian peasants off the land they'd inhabited for centuries, despite the fact that the Susuq family (rich Beiruti absentee landlords) <u>and</u> **Arthur Ruppin, head of the Jewish National Fund** tried to muscle him! But **al-'Asali** wasn't intimidated: he published an open letter (which he signed '**Saladin**', after the Arab hero who'd sent the Crusaders packing) in the important Damascus newspaper *al-Muqtabas*.

He published two more widely read articles. In these and other writings, al-'Asali linked the issue of peasant dispossession to patriotic themes, historically connecting the Palestinian people to the land, at least back to the time of Saladin—therefore, he argued, expelling the original peasant tenants was treason.

al-'Asali ran for office on a platform pledged to fight Zionism—and won.

Above all, it was the spectacle of Arab peasants resisting expulsion from their homes and lands to make room for foreign colonists that gave al-'Asali such appeal to Arabs. He was a defender of the poor, powerless and illiterate.

The Will of the People II

After the April 1920 anti-Zionist riots, the British sponsored a Commission of Inquiry to see why the Arabs were so unhappy. The Commission of Inquiry attributed the riots to **"Arab disappointment in the non-fulfillment of promises of independence and to their fear of economic & political subjugation to the Zionists."**

Arthur Ruppin, head of the Jewish National Fund and foremost land expert of the Jewish Agency, wasn't moved by the plight of the local people. "Land," he wrote, "is the most necessary thing for establishing our roots in Palestine. Since there are hardly any more arable unsettled lands in Palestine, we are bound in each case of the purchase of land and its settlement to remove the peasants who cultivated the land".

The Wailing Wall Incident

The Wailing Wall (or 'Western Wall') is a remnant of the 2nd Jewish Temple and an object of veneration to most Jews. To some it symbolizes the hope that the Temple will be rebuilt and the ancient Jewish rituals revived. However, the Western Wall also forms a part of the enclosure surrounding the historic Temple Mount on which stand the Dome of the Rock and al-Aqsa mosque, pilgrimage centers only slightly less holy to Muslims than Mecca and Medina. It had been a *waqf* (legally protected sacred site) since the time of Saladin. Muslims feared that Jewish actions before the Western Wall could lead to their pressing a claim to the Temple Mount.

In 1928 Jewish worshippers brought some benches to sit on and a screen to separate men from women. The police took them away several times, but the Jews kept putting them back. To Muslims this activity looked like an attempt by Jews to strengthen their claims to the Wall so they ran a road past it to distract the worshippers. Several fights broke out between Arabs and Jews. During the following year these escalated into a small civil war causing hundreds of casualties on both sides. When the Jews complained to the British authorities, Britain sent **yet another** Commission of Inquiry to ascertain the causes of the trouble.

W e Are the Aggressors...

The Will of the People III

In **1930** the British Colonial Secretary **Lord Passfield,** decided to clarify once and for all Britain's position on Palestine. **The Passfield White Paper** blamed the Jews for the trouble. The report bluntly stated that Jewish land purchases—primarily by the Jewish Agency— had left Arabs homeless on land they'd inhabited for centuries. The official British Statement of Policy declared that they would give priority to the Arabs who had lived in Palestine for hundreds of years. The report concluded: "**Arabs have come to see in Jewish immigration not only a menace to their livelihood but a possible overlord of the future.**"

(Perceptive little devils, weren't they?)

The Zionists were furious. They argued that Jewish immigrants, *actual* or *potential*, should be given priority over the Palestinian Arabs who had lived there for centuries!

(*That* is chutzpah!) (Of course, it's also racism.)

The Zionists nagged the British so relentlessly that, in **1931**, the British capitulated and *rescinded* the new Policy Statement! That, of course, convinced the Arabs that no matter what guarantees they were given in Palestine, the Zionists would twist someone's arm in London and have those guarantees annulled. All the promises of freedom and democracy were nothing but hot air. Arab delegates from 22 countries met to discuss the dangers of Zionism. The Arabs became more convinced than ever that they were never going to be treated fairly by the British.

The Arabs suspected that the English would keep them in colonial bondage until the Jews achieved a majority in Palestine and could set up their state.

That was in December of 1931. In 1933, Hitler came to power.

Ben Gurion Spills the Beans

- In 1933, 30,000 new Jewish immigrants come to Palestine.
- In 1934, 42,000 new Jewish immigrants come to Palestine.
- In 1935, 61,000 new Jewish immigrants come to Palestine.

The Arabs demanded the democratic institutions they'd been promised _and_ the right to set limits on immigration. The British proposed a legislative council to settle the disputes peaceably but the Zionists refused. The frustrated Arabs tried a general strike, then, when that failed, a rebellion.

MYTH: Regarding the semi-famous "Arab revolt of 1936-39"—it's generally assumed that the Arabs did most of the killing.
REALITY: I was at first shocked to learn that there were 329 Jews killed and 3,112 Arabs killed (_Britannica_, for some reason, excludes 1937) but after doing all this research I've realized that the ratio is usually about ten-to-one.

The redundant British sponsored another inquiry.
Maybe that's what made the Jewish terrorists go so crazy:
- In July of 1938, Irgun terrorists killed 76 Arabs by setting off bombs in markets and other public places.
- When an Irgun member was arrested by the British, the Irgun killed another 52 Arabs.
- In 1939, the British limited Jewish immigration to Palestine to 15,000 per year so the Irgun killed _another_ 27 Arabs!

In 1938, Ben Gurion gave Jewish leaders conniptions by telling the truth: "...in our political argument abroad, we minimize Arab opposition to us," but he said, "let us not ignore the truth among ourselves."

BenGurion said, **"we are the aggressors and they defend themselves..."**

Numbers

♦ Between 1900 and 1939, Zionist colonies in Palestine had increased from 22 to 200—nearly 1000 %
♦ From 1922 to 1939, Jewish landholdings in Palestine went from 148,000 acres to 383,350 acres—an increase of about 250 %
♦ From 1918 to 1939, Jewish population in Palestine had increased from 60,000 to 429,605—over 700 %.

Jews now constituted 28% of Palestine's population.

ANOTHER White Paper!

In May 1939 the British government issued a White Paper stating that, as far as Great Britain was concerned:

♦ They had already fulfilled their pledge to help establish a "Jewish national home" in Palestine.
♦ Indefinite Jewish immigration and transfer of Arab land to Jews were contrary to Article 22 of the Covenant of the League of Nations—and to British promises to the Arabs.
♦ Within the next five years, a maximum of 75,000 Jews would be allowed into Palestine; after 1944, Jewish immigration would be subject to Arab "acquiescence" (permission).
♦ An independent Palestinian state would be considered within the next 10 years [by 1949].

The enraged Zionists not only stepped up their terrorism, they began aiming more of it at the British. The Stern Gang murdered Lord Moyne, the British minister of state in Cairo, in November 1944.

Summary/recap

Up to World War II

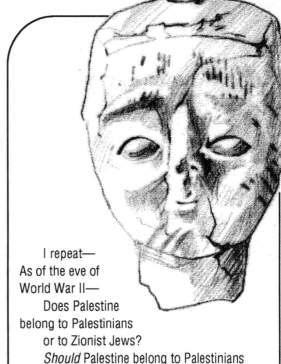

Where do we stand (regarding the Arab/Israeli conflict)**on the eve of W.W.II?**

The Arab/Israeli conflict is very specific—it is the conflict over Palestine.

As of the eve of World War II—
> Does Palestine belong to Palestinians or to Zionist Jews?
> *Should* Palestine belong to Palestinians or to Zionist Jews?

Overzealous supporters of Israel may say that I've asked the question in a 'loaded' way—but that's the first time the question has been asked in an UNloaded, *honest* way. Supporters of Israel torture, mangle and disguise the English language to keep from saying the dreaded "P"-word.

Actually, the *two* dreaded "P"-words: Palestinians *and* Palestine.

Ronald Reagan once gave Israel fits because he used the words "Palestinian" and "Homeland" in the same sentence!

I repeat—
As of the eve of World War II—
> Does Palestine belong to Palestinians or to Zionist Jews?
> *Should* Palestine belong to Palestinians or to Zionist Jews?

When the question is asked that straightforwardly, the answer is so obvious that it answers itself. Even so, let's go through the details:

When it Comes to Continuous Residence?

◆ Most Palestinians have lived in Palestine for several hundred (or several *thousand*) years. It is possible (or *likely*) that some Palestinians can trace their ancestry back to the ancient city of Jericho—*over 10,000 years ago!* (That's 6,000 years before Judaism was even a twinkle in Yaweh's eye!)

◆ As of the beginning of World War II: most of the Jews in Palestine had lived there between five and 35 years; they were from Tsarist Russia, had never been to the Middle East, and, like most Ashkenazi Jews, probably n*ever* had any Middle Eastern ancestry. Most of them loathed the heat, hated the Middle East and were hostile to and/or scared stiff of Arabs.

When it Comes to Will of the People?

No question.

The Zionist Arguments:

- Palestine is an empty desert—hogwash.
- There are no such things as Palestinians—word games...or worse. (Talk about denying people's identity!)
- Palestine is inhabited by people but not by a people.

What is the city but the people?

Coriolanus, Shakespeare

Bottom Line in Plain Old Streetcorner English

It isn't even close: the Palestinians deserve Palestine.

Please don't insult us with Word Games like "returning" to Israel.

(You can't *return* to a place where you haven't lived for 2,000 years.)

But you can *steal* it. After all, a lot of people think that Might is Right.

I won't try to impose my morality on you; all I insist on is Fairness: what's good for one side is good for the other.

But that poses problems. No Jew—and I hope no human being—will say that Might was Right for the Nazis to use against the Jews.

Menachem Begin was a fanatic who told the Truth exactly when he didn't mean to. "If this is Palestine and not the land of Israel," he said, "then you are conquerers and not tillers of the land. You are invaders. If this is Palestine, then it belongs to a people who lived here before you came."

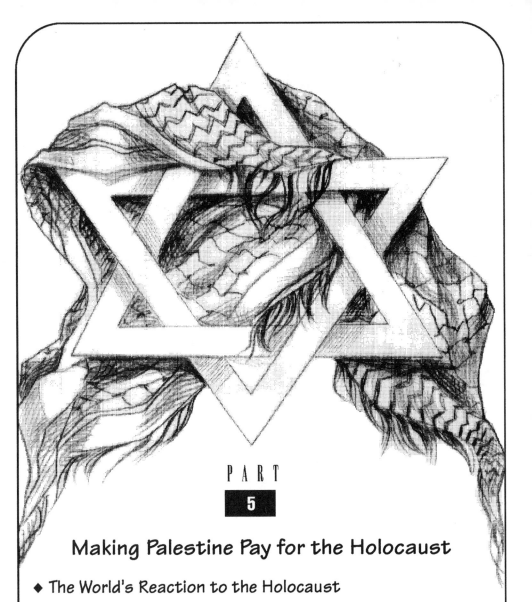

PART
5

Making Palestine Pay for the Holocaust

The World's Reaction to the Holocaust

On January 30, 1933, Hitler was appointed Chancellor of Germany. In 1933 the total U.S. immigration quota was 153,774; only 23,068 immigrants entered America but we made no special allowances for Jews.

Within the next few years, Germany barred Jews from decent jobs, deprived them of German citizenship, made it illegal for them to marry Germans, and searched back to 1800 for "Jewish blood" before issuing a 'certificate of purity'.

In March of 1938, ten days after the Nazis marched into Austria, the United States invited 33 countries to a conference on helping Jewish refugees from Germany.

(The Nazis laughed. They didn't believe we'd take in the Jews.)

In July, the representatives of 32 nations met in France for the eagerly awaited **Evian Conference**. Australia, New Zealand, Canada, Peru, Colombia,

Uruguay, and Venezuela said No. France, which had 200,000 refugees, said it had reached its saturation point. Argentina, with a population one-tenth of the United States, had already taken as many refugees as the U.S., so they begged off. Holland and Denmark were humane as always but they were already jammed full. England offered apologies. The United States, after having so generously called the conference, offered nothing but to honor the quota we already had.

The Nazis called us a bunch of hypocrites, had a good laugh, and continued imprisoning and brutalizing Jews before offering to release them if they relinquished their property and left the country within six weeks. 3,000 Jews a day waited in vain for visas at the American consulate in Vienna.

I am not easy on England because

their sliminess contributed greatly to the Arab/Israeli conflict, but when it comes to World War II, the British were the only ones with the balls to stand up to Hitler. If the Japanese hadn't attacked us at Pearl Harbor, I'm not sure if America would have ever entered the war.

In November of 1938, the Nazis burned down every synagogue in Germany, shattered the windows of every Jewish business, and took 20,000 Jews to concentration camps. It was worse in Vienna.

The following April, the Congress of the United States began hearings on whether or not to admit 20,000 Jewish children—*children*— into the U.S. to escape Hitler. Congress voted No.

In 1939, a ship called the *St. Louis* left Germany with 930 Jews, most of whom had U.S. immigration permits with numbers like you take in a butcher shop. When the ship got to America we wouldn't take them because their numbers hadn't come up yet. As the *St. Louis* headed back to Germany, *The New York Times* wrote a heartbreaking editorial about "man's inhumanity to man" but did not in any way suggest that the *St. Louis* be allowed to dock anywhere in the huge, bighearted country of America.

Finally, the ship was allowed to dock in Belgium.

In 1941, when the massacre of Jews had spread to Rumania, a Turkish minister in Rumania came up with a plan to save 300,000 Rumanian Jews. When the Turkish minister asked the United States for help, the U.S. said No.

In 1941, instead of making it easier for Jewish refugees to get into the U.S., America passed new immigration laws making it almost impossible for Jews to get into the U.S.

In the spring of 1942 the Nazis installed gas chambers in Polish concentration camps. The lethal gas they used was called 'Zyklon B'.

(Before that, they had used mobile gas vans, into which they packed 90 Jews at a time and asphyxiated them with carbon monoxide.)

In the summer of 1942 the Nazis arrested 20,000 Jews in Paris, then five days after Paris the Nazis resumed the cold slaughter of the remaining 380,000 inhabitants of the Warsaw ghetto and in Latvia the Nazis machine-gunned 25,000 Jews and exterminated another 50,000 Jews in Lwow and, in one of those acts that insult everything human, the Nazis used the corpses of Jewish human beings for fertilizer.

The Nazis used bulldozers to push the bodies of dead Jews into holes.

It's not that there were no heroes. There were, but they were few and far between and they came from funny places like Sweden.

Raoul Wallenberg was a Swede who had risked his life to save Jews from concentration camps. When the war was over and the Jews were safe, they honored Wallenberg by naming a street after him in Budapest and paid tribute to him with a prayer that included these words:

The time of horror is still fresh in our memory, when the Jews of this country were like hunted animals, when thousands of Jewish prisoners were in the temples preparing for death. We recall all the atrocities of the concentration camps, the departure of trains crammed with people who were to die.... But we also remember one of the greatest heroes of those terrible times: the Secretary of the Royal Swedish Legation, who defied the intruding government and its armed executioners. We witnessed the redemption of prisoners and the relief of sufferers when Mr. Wallenberg came among the persecuted to help. In a superhuman effort, not yielding to fatigue and exposing himself to all sorts of dangers, he brought home children who had been dragged away and he liberated aged parents.

We shall never forget him and shall be forever grateful to him and to the Swedish nation, because it was the Swedish flag which warranted the undisturbed slumber of thousands of Jews in protected houses. He was a righteous man. God bless him.

There was another Swede, **Count Folke Bernadotte**, who saved Jews from concentration camps. He was the head of the Swedish Red Cross—and the former Head of the Swedish Boy Scouts—so he hardly seemed like the kind of guy who'd go up against the Nazis, but he faced down Himmler, the head of the Gestapo and saved 20,000 Jews from the concentration camps. They thanked him in a different way.

he Unbelievable Zionist Reaction to the Holocaust

I believe I've made the point that, despite what was being done to Jews in Hitler's Europe, none of the holy Western democracies welcomed Jews into their countries. Indeed, toward the end of World War II, America passed new immigration laws making it MORE difficult for Jews to enter the U.S.

But the question remains, **Why didn't influential Jews persuade the U.S. to open its doors to save Jews from the camps?**

Because—as horrible as it is to admit—Zionists cared more about creating a Jewish state in Palestine than they did about saving Jews from Hitler.

In his book, *America and the Survivors of the Holocaust*, Leonard Dinnerstein writes, "Unspoken publicly, but in the air privately, was the Zionist concern that fewer European Jews would resettle in Israel if the possibility existed of getting to the United States."

Not only did Zionists NOT work to get Jewish refugees into America, they worked to keep them OUT. Morris Ernst, President Roosevelt's advisor, wrote in 1948, of his shock at the refusal of American Jewish leaders to give "these beaten people of Europe a choice," instead of offering them only the option of emigrating to Palestine. Ernst suggested a program that "would free us from the hypocrisy of closing our own doors while making sanctimonious demands on the Arabs."

He wrote that he "was amazed and even felt insulted when active Jewish leaders decried, sneered and then attacked me as if I were a traitor" for suggesting that the survivors of the Holocaust be allowed to emigrate to the United States.

A few good books on a bad subject:
- *America and the Survivors of the Holocaust*, by Leonard Dinnerstein
- *The Zionist Connection* by Alfred Lilienthal
- *The Politics of Rescue* by Henry L. Feingold
- *American Jewry and the Holocaust* by Yehuda Bauer
- *The Holocaust Victims Accuse: Documents & Testimony on Jewish War Criminals* by the Neturei Karta, an organization of anti-Zionist Jews that has its roots in the pre-Zionist Jewish settlement and that now supports secular democracy rather than a Jewish state.

The most unforgivable things were done in the DP camps after the war.

After World War II, American soldiers in Germany presided over camps full of Jewish 'displaced persons' [DPs] waiting for the chance to resettle in America, Europe, or the Middle East. The organization that officially helped the DPs emigrate was the Jewish Agency but, after a certain point, the **Irgun** (the terrorist group led by Menachem Begin) and the **Stern** gang (the terrorist group led by Yitzhak Shamir) began "recruiting" in the DP camps.

From the official report of the Office of the Military Government for Germany—U.S. (OMGUS), dated January 10, 1948:

Tensions and clashes in the Jewish DP camps are now on the increase. They are spreading to various parts of the U.S. zone and are gaining momentum. In the back of it all is an attempt and determination of the 'Irgun Zevai Leumi' to gain control of the camp administrations and institutions.

They find it hard however to take over committees that are democratically elected and are working under an Army charter and subject to public control and scrutiny. Irgun, therefore, seems to concentrate on the DP police force. This is an old technique in Eastern Europe and in all police states. By controlling the police, a small, unscrupulous group of determined people can impose its will on a peaceful and inarticulate majority; it is done by threats, intimidation, by violence and if need be by bloodshed....they have embarked upon a course of violence within the camps.

Zionist Jews threatened, terrorized, and brutalized the Jews who'd just survived the Holocaust to 'persuade' them to go to Israel. The thought of it angers me more than anything I know. If you can stand to read more, by all means, pick up the book *Taking Sides* by Stephen Green.

The Haganah archives contain the names of 40 Jews who were killed by Irgun and the Stern Gang in other situations.

The United Nations Insult to Democracy

During WW-II, 12,000 Palestinians enlisted in the British Army to help fight the Nazis.

Palestine, a country of only two million people, accepted more Jewish refugees than any country in the world.

After the war, President Truman, who had not invited any of the Holocaust victims to America, joined the Zionists in self-righteously demanding the immediate admission of 100,000 more Jews into Palestine. This time, the Arabs said NO—it was their country!

The Americans told the British to force the Arabs to acquiesce.

The touchy British, apparently still miffed over the fact that the Irgun had killed Lord Moyne (British Minister of State) said, "As soon as the Zionists disband their 65,000 man underground."

The Zionists replied by blowing up the King David Hotel in Jerusalem, killing 91 Britons and several Jews.

The British, sick of it all (and probably impervious to the fact that they caused it) gave the problem to the newly formed United Nations.

America's Affront to Democracy

In November of 1947, under great pressure from America (Truman, the underdog in the upcoming election, was grovelling for the Jewish vote), the United Nations General Assembly recommended that Palestine be "provisionally partitioned" into a part Arab, part Jewish state.

The Palestinians, who, even after 40 years of Zionist propaganda and forced immigration, *still* had a huge two-to-one majority—1,269,000 Arabs to 678,000 Jews—protested mightily. More precisely, ALL of the Islamic countries protested. (*'So this is what you mean by democracy!'*) The Arabs asked to query the International Court of Justice on the right of the United Nations to partition a country against the will of its people but they were voted down. The great democracies of the West had actually given away Palestine without so much as consulting the Palestinians! To add insult to injury, the Jews owned only 7% of Palestine, but they were given 55% of the land! The swindled Palestinians began fighting.

America's (post-election) Attack of Conscience

Early in March 1948 the United States suddenly 'realized' its affront to democratic principles and went on record opposing the forcible partition of Palestine. On March 19 the U.S. called for the suspension of the United Nations' efforts to partition Palestine and on March 30 the U.S. called for an immediate truce and further discussion by the United Nations General Assembly.
The Zionists, insisting that partition was binding and anxious about the change in U.S. policy, decided to ignore legal niceties.
The Zionists intensified the fighting.

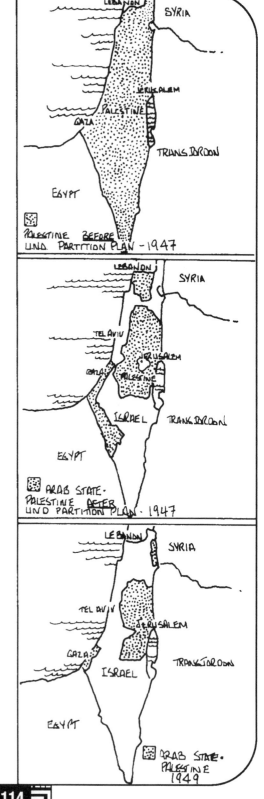

Ethnic Cleansing

"It was a miraculous clearing of the land."
Chaim Weizmann, 1st president of Israel

"As in Deir Yassin, so everywhere."

1948, April: Zionist (Irgun) terror squads massacred 254 Palestinians in the village of Deir Yassin. Two hundred and fifty-four Arab women, children and old men were butchered by the Zionists while the young Arab men worked in the fields. Unborn children were killed inside the guts of their murdered mothers. There was talk of hands being cut off, and of children being blinded but that was hard to prove because most of the bodies were thrown down a well. (The noble Zionists also dynamited houses, looted, and raped but that's hardly worth mentioning.)

Within a few days, as the Zionists had hoped, half a million Palestinians fled their country in terror to make room for Israel.

That was in 1948, in the sad dead village of Deir Yassin.

The Irgun command sent a message to its men: **"As in Deir Yassin, so everywhere"**.

The massacre at Deir Yassin was led by Menachem Begin, the twice-elected Premier of Israel.

Deir Yassin is now Givat Shaul Beth [part of Jerusalem]; in 1980, what was left of the ruins of Deir Yassin were bulldozed and made into a settlement for Orthodox Jews. The streets were named after the Irgun units that had massacred the Palestinians and the Deir Yassin cemetery was bulldozed to make way for a new Jewish highway.

That is how Israel was "established"—every home, every tree, every square foot of it.

And **that** is the plain brutal truth.

The refusal to face that truth (and the truths that follow from it) is the main reason that Israel never gets any closer to peace with the Arabs—and why, more and more, America is suckered into conflicts in the Middle East that have nothing to do with American interests.
But we'll save all that for a later chapter...on Peace.

Don't make the mistake of thinking that Deir Yassin was an isolated case where a few Jewish individuals got overheated—it was Zionist policy.

Deir Yassin was one of hundreds of Zionist "land-clearing operations".

(When Russians massacre Jews it is a "pogrom"; when Jews massacre Palestinians, it is a "land-clearing operation".)

Israel's "land-clearing operations" were so successful that 780,000 Palestinians fled their country in terror. A few weeks after Deir Yassin, Israel declared itself a country.

Declared <u>itself</u> a country? Can one do that?

The Arabs thought not. That is why they all entered the war.

On May 14, 1948, in Tel Aviv, Jewish leaders led by David Ben Gurion, chairman of the Jewish Agency and head of the Zionist workers movement, proclaimed the State of Israel. Nahum Goldmann (President of the World Zionist Organization from 1956-68) opposed the decision to establish the State of Israel, on the assumption that a peaceful diplomatic settlement might be possible.

Jewish Leaders ignored him.

On the day that Israel declared itself a country, the American delegate to the United Nations was going on record as OPPOSING a Jewish state in Palestine!

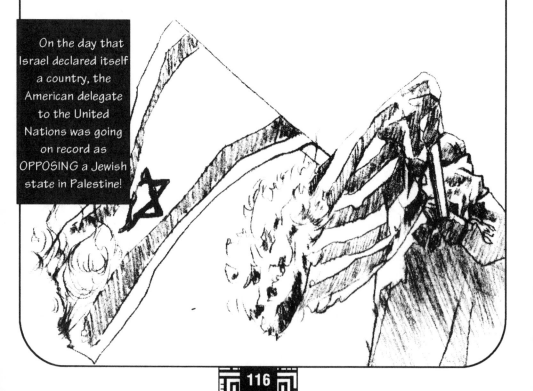

The Former Head of the Boy Scouts vs The Future Prime Minister of Israel

On May 20, the United Nations appointed **Count Folke Bernadotte** as mediator between Israel and the Arabs. (Jews were pleased: Count Bernadotte was the head of the Swedish Red Cross who had risked his life to save thousands of Jews from concentration camps.) Count Bernadotte did everything in his power to stop the war between Zionists and Arabs.

I say 'Zionists' because Bernadotte insisted that there was not yet any such country as Israel.

He said that the November 1947 U.N. partition of Palestine was "provisional", *temporary*, intended only to see if partition was a feasible solution and, as any fool could now see, it was *not* feasible. Bernadotte reminded them that UN General Assembly resolutions were **not** binding. Bernadotte insisted that if the Zionists *accepted* the United Nations' authority, then they must return to the U.N. to establish where—and IF—Israel would be; if the Zionists *rejected* the U.N.'s authority, then they must ALSO reject the U.N.'s authority to partition Palestine in the first place. Therefore, in either case, as of this moment, there IS no Israel. (The logic is flawless: the only way to refute that argument is with a very large gun.)

On September 15, in the 'Bernadotte Plan', Count Bernadotte proposed that, IF Zionists were eventually given part of Palestine, in the interest of human decency, Palestinian refugees must be given two options: *One*, they should be allowed to **return** to their homes in Palestine at **any time** in the future; *Two*, if they chose not to return to Palestine, they should be **compensated** by Israel for all that was taken from them.

In summary: *ALL* Palestinians, at *ANY* time, should have the choice of either **Return** or **Compensation**!

With Count Bernadotte's war record, it would have been silly to accuse him of antiSemitism.

So the next day the Zionists murdered him.

You think this is bad? It gets worse: Count Bernadotte, who had saved 20,000 Jews from Hitler, was killed on orders from **Yitzhak Shamir**, whose Stern Gang had offered to help the Nazis! (Doubting Thomases should consult the ugly January, 1983 article in HA'ARETZ, the Israeli N.Y. TIMES.)

A 1941 Stern Gang proposal even offered to form a Jewish state "on a national and totalitarian basis, which will establish relations with the German Reich" and protect Nazi interests in the Middle East!)

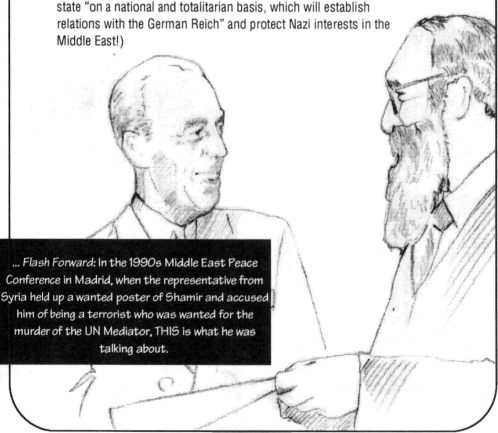

... *Flash Forward:* In the 1990s Middle East Peace Conference in Madrid, when the representative from Syria held up a wanted poster of Shamir and accused him of being a terrorist who was wanted for the murder of the UN Mediator, THIS is what he was talking about.

1948-49:

To the Zionists—
The War of
Independence
To Palestinians—
al-Nakba—
"the Disaster"

In November 1947, the General Assembly of the United Nations had recommended the partition of mandatory Palestine into a Jewish and an Arab state. War broke out immediately.

But what happened is a little—a *lot*—different than you've heard.

The 'mythological' version goes something like this:

The Jews have four or five thousand Palmach troops and a paper army of fifty thousand in the Haganah, but they have only ten thousand rifles. The Macabees can put a thousand men out, no more, with light arms. They have no artillery, their air force is three Piper Cubs, and their navy is those illegal-immigrant runners tied up at Haifa. The Jews are outnumbered in soldiers forty to one, in population a hundred to one, in equipment a thousand to one, and in area five thousand to one.

from Exodus by Leon Uris

David and Goliath all over again, right? Right. Except that it was the other way around.

In their propaganda the Zionists had always depicted themselves as the poor-little-underdog Jews who didn't stand a chance against the big-ugly-Goliath-Arabs. But from the moment they provoked that first war with the Arabs, the Zionists/Jews/Israelis knew they had an army bigger and stronger than all of the Arabs combined. In the last few years, books have been published and secret documents declassified that, at long last, give us an honest picture of Israel. And the picture isn't pretty.

Declassified documents from the U.S. National Archives reveal:

◆ The CIA's 1947 assessment: Zionist leadership, taking advantage of world sympathy for the Holocaust, was recklessly provoking the Arabs and was endangering both Palestinian Jews and the strategic interests of the U.S.

◆ The Joint Chief of Staff's 1948 listing of the five Zionist objectives, the last two being:

> ❥ the expansion of Israel into Jordan and parts of Lebanon & Syria.
> ❥ establishing Jewish military & economic control over the **entire Middle East**.

◆ In mid-June of 1948, a truce was imposed on Jews and Arabs. Every United States government agency in the Middle East documented the Jewish truce violations.

◆ The U.S. Military Attache' in Baghdad reported that King Abdullah of Transjordan had to cease his Army's practice of returning Jewish female prisoners of war under flags of truce because of repeated instances in which Jewish forces had fired on the Arabs on their way back to their own lines.

◆ During late June and early July, the U.S. Consuls in Jerusalem and Haifa reported massive amounts of new arms and thousands of trained soldiers being flown in from Eastern Europe, using Arab prisoner-of-war labor to build new fortifications, and forced movements of Arab civilian populations, all violations of the UN truce agreement and/or the Geneva Conventions.

In his 1987 book, *The Birth of Israel: Myths and Realities*, Zionist historian Simha Flapan writes, "like most Israelis, I had always been under the influence of certain myths that had become accepted as historical truth."

One of the myths that Flapan exposes is that the Arabs started the war. Flapan says that the "Arabs had agreed to a last-minute American proposal for a three-month truce on the condition that Israel temporarily postpone its Declaration of Independence. Israel's provisional government rejected the American proposal by a slim majority of 6 to 4."

Ronald Bleier, in the Jan/Feb 1993, *Lies of our Times*, writes, "In the war between the stronger Jewish forces and the less prepared Arab community, parallels can be drawn to the ethnic cleansing that is going on in Bosnia. Like the Serbs today, the Jewish forces generally did everything they could to force the Palestinians to flee their cities, town, and villages."

On May 18, four days after the fighting between the Zionists and the Arabs started, the U.S. Army Intelligence Division sent a memo to the Chief of Staff stating that the **combined** army of **all Arab forces** totalled about 30,000 ill-equipped, poorly trained men. The Zionist army of over 90,000 not only **outnumbered the Arabs three to one**, but they had modern weaponry, including up-to-date fighter and bomber airplanes with well-trained pilots. The U.S. Army, British Intelligence, and the CIA all agreed: the Zionists had an army bigger stronger and infinitely more advanced than all the Arabs combined. It would be no contest.

By the time the war was over, Israel had three-fourths of Palestine, twice as much land as proposed by the UN. No peace treaties were signed, however, and no Arab state granted Israel diplomatic recognition. In January 1949 David Ben Gurion was elected the nation's first prime minister and Chaim Weizmann became president. Israel was admitted to the UN in May 1949.

NOTE: The United States' recognition of Israel was made contingent on Israel's acceptance of the Palestinians' right of Return or Compensation—which Israel has still not granted.

PART
6

David is Goliath—Wars with Cute Names

◆ The 50s: Unit 101, Qibya, the Lavon Affair,
  the 1956 Suez War

◆ The 1967 "Six Day War"

◆ The 1973 "Yom Kippur War"

The 50s: Unit 101, Qibya, the Lavon Affair, the 1956 Suez War

1950: Jordan annexes West Bank; Egypt seizes Gaza.

1951: King Abdallah of Jordan is assasinated by a 19-year-old Palestinian. Israel rejects UN peace plan accepted by Egypt, Syria, Lebanon, & Jordan.

Unit 101 & Qibya

Moshe Dayan, head of the Operations Dept. of Israel's Army, decided that his army was getting sloppy, "lowering its fighting standards." Dayan, who recognized talent when he saw it, knew that Ariel Sharon was exactly what the IDF (Israeli Defense Forces) needed. Ariel Sharon formed a special commando force, Unit 101.

Unit 101 specialized in night raids and phony "reprisal raids." General Dayan had said that Israel must "invent dangers" and "adopt the method of provocation and revenge." So, Sharon, who was a quick learner, had his men provoke neighboring Arabs into doing something petty, then used that as an excuse to sneak across the border at night and kill a few Arabs.

In *Sharon, an Israeli Caesar*, by Uzi Benziman, we get a pretty clear picture of Ariel Sharon: Sharon, personally, slit the throats of sleeping Egyptian soldiers. Sharon's men killed so many Syrians that Ben Gurion, that master of doublespeak, called the action "too successful". Sharon bitched out one of his officers for not killing two old Arabs when they had the opportunity. Sharon laughed as a junior officer tormented an old Arab and then shot him at close range. Sharon ordered his men to ambush and kill two Jordanian women on their way to a well.

Sounds like quite a guy!

On October 14-15, 1953 Ariel Sharon and his Unit 101 sneaked across the border into the West Bank Jordanian village of Qibya and slaugh-tered 53 Lebanese and Palestinian civilians. Moshe Dayan thought that Sharon's Unit 101 "operated with such brilliance that its achievements set an example to all the other formations in the army." Still, slaughtering 53 innocent civilians attracted a little too much attention so, Ben Gurion covered it up with a nice lie.

The next part takes place in Egypt.

Egypt

Size: 386,900 sq.miles.

Population: 38 million: Arab, 99%; Muslim, 92.9%; Christian, 6.7%

Who Rules: The President, chosen by the National Assembly and confirmed by plebiscite. The legislature has 350 elected members.

How Created: Egypt goes back 6,000 years—the longest history of any Middle Eastern civilization [along with Mesopotamia]. Napoleon conquered Egypt in 1798. The British and Turks drove out the French in 1805 and Muhammad Ali, an Albanian, ruled. After the opening of the Suez Canal in 1869, the British took a profound interest in Egypt. When nationalist politics interfered with British interests, they sent in the army [1914]. After Egypt's independence [1936], Britain, considerate as always, stayed on to look after the canal. In 1952 the military overthrew the King and Gamal Abdul Nasser became Egypt's leader. Nasser nationalized the Suez Canal and forced Britain to withdraw troops from Egypt. He was considered the first real Arab nationalist leader.

The Levon Affair

Around the time that **Gamal Abdul Nasser** became Egypt's leader, David Ben Gurion had decided (partly out of spite) to step down as Prime Minister of Israel and let Moshe Sharett see if he could do a better job. Sharett was less of a 'Hawk' than Ben Gurion and, by 1954, had reached the point where he was on the verge of signing a peace treaty with Nasser of Egypt.

Nasser is usually depicted as one of the bad guys. Recently declassified State Department documents indicate the exact opposite. Documentary evidence [1948-54] shows Nasser expressing tolerance and respect for Israel to CIA officials, members of British Parliament, and two American Ambassadors. In **October 1954** Nassar became one of the only heads of state to refuse military aid from the U.S. He preferred economic aid.

Then, in 1954, Israeli terrorists attacked American installations in Egypt!

Then the Israelis rigged it so the attacks would be blamed on Egyptians?

Then the Israelis got caught and put in Egyptian prisons.

. . .all of which convinced Egypt's Nasser that the Israelis couldn't be trusted, so he broke off the peace talks and took weapons from whomever offered them—including the Soviets.

Ben Gurion blamed the blundering terrorists on his Defense Minister, **Pinchas Lavon**—but several years later, Lavon found documents that proved Ben Gurion was behind it!

Ben Gurion's motive was simple: he and Moshe Dayan wanted a war with Egypt and Sharett's peace talks might deprive them of it.

In June 1955, Moshe Sharett [in his Diaries] wrote: '**Dayan said, "above all, let us hope for a new war with the Arab countries, so that we may finally get rid of our troubles and acquire space."**'

Another of Sharett's Diary entries for June 1955: '**Ben Gurion himself said it would be worthwhile to pay an Arab a million pounds to start a war. What a slip of the tongue!**'

The Sinai Campaign

In 1956, Israel attacked Egypt, then hoodwinked much of the world into thinking that Egypt was the aggressor. For the last year, every Intelligence source available had confirmed the fact that there was no way the Israelis could lose that war. Even if all the other Arab armies joined to help Egypt, Israel's Army was bigger and badder and more technologically advanced than all of them combined. The reason Israel was so antsy to attack Egypt is that Nasser, with Soviet help, was beginning to build a fair sized army. So Israel went in and demolished it in a couple days.

In addition, thousands of Arabs—citizens of Israel—were expelled from Israel's Galilee region during the 1956 attack on Egypt. This previously unknown fact was revealed by Prime Minister Yitzhak Rabin, who at the time was commander of Israel's northern region. He said that 3,000 to 5,000 Arabs—Israeli citizens—were expelled by the Israeli Army to Syria at that time.

After the war, the occupying Israeli Army slaughtered hundreds of Palestinians and robbed homes in the Gaza Strip.

The 1967 "Six Day War"

1964: First Summit Meeting of Arab leaders in Cairo. The PLO is created.

Back in the days when Lyndon Johnson was running for office in Texas, one of his aides asked LBJ why he had publicly accused his opponent of having sexual relations with pigs.

> "Did he really —'make love'— to pigs?" the aide asked.
> "Not as I know of," Johnson replied.
> "Then why accuse him of it?"
> "B'cause from now on,"

Johnson said, "he'll have to spend all his time denying it."

MYTH: The 1967 "Six Day War"

Israel was sitting there minding her own beeswax when 250 million Arabs started sneaking toward her borders with the intention of driving her into the sea so against zillion-to-one odds teensy weensy little Israel at the last instant launched a Pre-Emptive Strike and just like David miraculously frigged Goliath itsy bitsy little Israel Michael Jordaned out a last second underdog victory against the Devils of the Desert.

REALITY: The 1967 "Six Day Turkey Shoot"

There was a war, it started on June 5, it lasted six days, and Israel won it. The rest is pure fertilizer. Two Israeli Generals and one Prime Minister get us a little closer to the truth:

◆ Menachem Begin [Prime Minister of Israel]: "The Egyptian Army concentrations in the Sinai approaches do not prove that Nasser was really about to attack us. We must be honest with ourselves. We decided to attack him."

◆   General Rabin [IDF Chief of Staff in 1967]: "I do not think Nasser wanted war. The two divisions he sent into the Sinai, on May 14, would not have been sufficient to launch an offensive against Israel. He knew it and we knew it."

◆   General Peled: "The thesis that claimed genocide was suspended above our heads in June 1967, and that Israel was fighting for its very existence was only a bluff."

Author Stephen Green follows the truth wherever it leads:

"The third major Middle East war was inevitable from around 1965 until it occurred in June of 1967, and the outcome of that war was absolutely certain."

—from *Taking Sides* by **Stephen Green**

Mr. Green quotes source after source from our State Department's archives that come to the same conclusions:

◆   Israel is looking for an excuse to attack the Arabs.

◆   Israel's Army is *much* stronger than all the Arab armies combined.

◆   When the war starts—not *if*, *when*—Israel will win it within a week.

Walt Rostow, Lyndon Johnson's closest foreign policy adviser, kept LBJ informed. On the first day of the "war" Rostow's report was accompanied by a note: "Mr. President: Herewith the account, with a map, of the first day's turkey shoot. W.W. Rostow."

Israel had carried out a massive sneak attack, destroying 300 Egyptian airplanes (while they were still on the ground) in the first three hours, then after the Arabs agreed to a U.S./UN/Russian-sponsored ceasefire, Israel kept gobbling up territory. Israel didn't even start on the Syrians until after the ceasefire, after which Poor Little Israel spent two full days blowing the hell out of various parts of Syria.

The Coach's Son

Calls for a cease-fire started pouring in to the United Nations "almost as soon as the fighting." So why did it take the UN two days to issue a cease-fire order?

Because America's delegation to the UN, led by Ambassador Arthur Goldberg, resisted any cease-fire resolution that would (a) brand Israel as the aggressor or (b) include a demand for troop withdrawl to the June 4 borders."

Israel was the aggressor. Ambassador Goldberg *knew* that Israel was the aggressor.

Yet he stalled the cease-fire for two full days so that:

1. Israel's lie would go on record as The Official Truth.

2. Israel would have time to kill more

Egyptians, steal more territory, and get some momentum on killing Syrians and stealing Syrian territory.

Do you know what really bothers me about that?

Arthur Goldberg was Jewish. Arthur, baby, the coach is supposed to be *harder* on his son, he's not supposed to kill all the quarterbacks so his son can make the team.

By the time the "Six Day Turkey Shoot" was over, Israel had *stolen*— 'annexed' is a bullshit word—*stolen* the Sinai Peninsula, the Gaza Strip, East Jerusalem, and the West Bank.

And conned the world into thinking that the Arabs were the aggressors!

Since the victims were "only" Arabs, maybe that story amuses you.

I guarantee you this one won't amuse you:

> **On June 8, 1967, Israeli planes attacked the American electronics ship Liberty in international waters. They lied and said it was an accident but it wasn't an accident—they attacked the Liberty again and again, over a span of hours. They even shot lifeboats out of the water.**

The Israelis killed 34 American crewmen and wounded 171 others. They did it intentionally and our government knows it. (It's in the State Department records!)

After the 67 War, half-a-million Arabs fled or were expelled from the conquered territories! (More 'Land-clearing operations'.)

The UN had provisionally 'loaned' Israel 5,000 square miles of Palestine.

By 1955, Israel occupied 8,000 square miles of Palestine.

After the 1967 war, Israel occupied 30,000 square miles.

The Dead...
Do you know how many Israelis were killed in the Six Day War?
275 – What a hideous, horrible, stupid waste of human life.
Do you know how many Egyptians were killed in the Six Day war?
12,000.
The Israelis killed two thousand Egyptians per day.

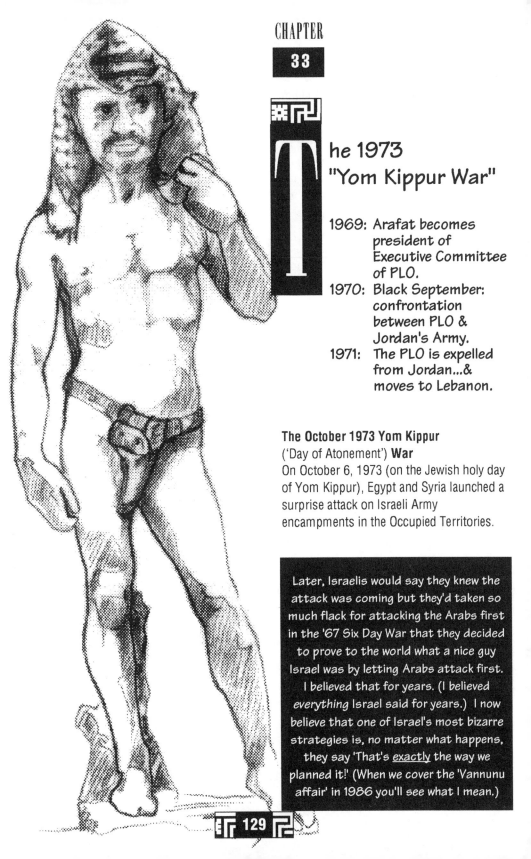

The 1973 "Yom Kippur War"

1969: Arafat becomes president of Executive Committee of PLO.

1970: Black September: confrontation between PLO & Jordan's Army.

1971: The PLO is expelled from Jordan...& moves to Lebanon.

The October 1973 Yom Kippur
('Day of Atonement') **War**
On October 6, 1973 (on the Jewish holy day of Yom Kippur), Egypt and Syria launched a surprise attack on Israeli Army encampments in the Occupied Territories.

Later, Israelis would say they knew the attack was coming but they'd taken so much flack for attacking the Arabs first in the '67 Six Day War that they decided to prove to the world what a nice guy Israel was by letting Arabs attack first.

I believed that for years. (I believed *everything* Israel said for years.) I now believe that one of Israel's most bizarre strategies is, no matter what happens, they say 'That's <u>exactly</u> the way we planned it!' (When we cover the 'Vannunu affair' in 1986 you'll see what I mean.)

For the first week of the war, Israel's situation looked worse every day. Israeli counter-attacks failed, the Syrians and Egyptians were fighting an inspired war, and the IDF (Israeli Defense Forces) were suffering great losses.

General Ariel Sharon, whose big mouth and sadistic personality had kept him from being promoted to Israeli Chief of Staff a few months earlier, had quit the Army in a snit. On his good days Ariel Sharon was a military genius with a flair for the dramatic who almost always went too far—exactly what you need when you're getting stomped by Syrians & Egyptians.

After the Egyptians had beaten the IDF back across the Suez Canal and showed no signs of stopping, Ariel Sharon was called back into the Army.

In a move that most military historians consider the slickest maneuver in Israel's military history, Sharon befuddled the Egyptians by breaking through their advancing lines and using half of his men to attack the Egyptians from the rear and the other half, believe it or not, to march on Cairo!

By the time nervous Henry Kissinger bulldogged Israel's government into stopping Sharon's outrageously balsy advance, he was within 63 miles of taking Cairo—and we were chest to chest with the Russians!

The war brought severe internal criticism in Israel. The findings of a commission of inquiry led to the resignation of Golda Meir's **Labor** government in April 1974. The only Israeli hero to emerge from the '73 War was Ariel Sharon. After the war the people of Israel carried him on their shoulders, chanting, **"Sharon, King of Israel. Sharon, King of Israel."**

The 1973 War was the **only** clear case of an Arab attack on Israel. . .but even then there were monumentally extenuating circumstances.

Egypt & Syria did **NOT** attack Israel.
◆ They attacked IDF forces, but **ONLY** in the **Occupied Territories** in the **Sinai** & **Golan Heights**—which, according to the United Nations, Israel was supposed to have unoccupied 6 years earlier.
◆ The attacks came only after Israel had rebuffed several Arab attempts at peaceful settlements, including Sadat's 1971 offer* to Israel of a **Full Peace Treaty** with better conditions than the one Israel finally accepted in 1979.

*Noam Chomsky, in his brave truthful book *The Fateful Triangle*, says that Sadat's peace offer is so well known in Israel that Israeli newspapers refer to it as "Sadat's *famous* 1971 peace offer"
—but **The New York Times** refused/refuses to even mention it!
(Shouldn't there be a law against that? Withholding important information in a democracy is like 'stuffing' the ballot box.)

The Dead. . .
Do you know how many Israelis were killed in the Yom Kippur War?
2,552—What a hideous, horrible, stupid waste of human life.
Do you know how many Arabs were killed in the Yom Kippur War?
15,000.

Jordan
Size: about the size of Indiana.
Population: 4,000,000: 93% Sunni Muslim; 6% Christian
How Created: After World War I, England chopped off part of Palestine and part of Syria...and gave it to Abdullah, the grandfather of Jordan's current King Hussein—and a descendant of the Prophet Muhammad.

Blaming the Victims — I

- ◆ Palestinians & the PLO

- ◆ Israel's Dismemberment of Lebanon: Part 1

Palestinians & the PLO

"It is not as though there was a Palestinian people and we came and threw them out and took their country away from them. They did not exist."
Golda Meir, prime minister of Israel—1969

After 20 Years of Land Clearing Operations

Israel's 1947-49 Land-Clearing Operations not only created 780,000 Palestinian refugees, but Zionist terror squads also totally destroyed 416 Palestinian villages, and seized all their lands and assets. Three to five thousand more Palestinians—Arab citizens of Israel—were thrown out during the 1956 Sinai campaign. And after the '67 War, another <u>half-million</u> Palestinians fled or were expelled from the Occupied Territories by the Israeli Army.

After twenty years of Israeli Land-Clearing Operations, two million Palestinians, run out of their own country, lived in Jordan, Lebanon, and Syria, most of them as refugees, longing for home, incredibly confused at how the world could consider *them* the bad guys—and even more confused by the ridiculous Jewish assertion they did not exist!

The PLO

In 1964, at a summit meeting of Arab leaders in Cairo, Egypt, the **PLO** (Palestine Liberation Organization) was created. The PLO's charter stated that the Palestinian people had a right to self-determination and that they were willing to fight to regain their homeland (with borders stipulated by the original British mandate). The PLO's charter stated that Jews of Palestinian origin could continue to live within the liberated country of Palestine, a country that would be <u>secular</u> and <u>democratic</u>. In the early days, the PLO was run by politicians so it didn't accomplish much of anything.

Arafat & Fatah

About a year later, **Yasir Arafat** started his own group, called *Fatah*. Arafat believed that Palestinians couldn't count on anyone but themselves—and that the only realistic way of getting Palestine back was the same way they'd lost it, by armed struggle. There was also the matter of pride: Arafat couldn't bear to see his people thought of by the world as pitiful refugees standing in line for United Nations' handouts.

In 1965 and 1966, Arafat's *Fatah* (armed by Syria) began launching attacks on Israel from Jordan. Then, in 1967, after the Arabs' humiliating defeat in the

> A similar 'I'd-rather-kick-your-ass-and-take-it-from-you-than-beg-you-for-it' pride was at the center of Malcolm X's great appeal.

Six Day War, Arafat's *Fatah* was the only thing they could be a little proud of, so the PLO welcomed Arafat. Arafat, slipping from town to town on his motorbike, almost single-handedly created a Palestinian underground in the Occupied Territories after the '67 War. Young men, eager to reclaim Arab pride, flocked to become *fedayeen*— 'commandos'.

To stop Arafat's Jordan-based PLO attacks, Israel started one of its ugliest strategies: instead of attacking the PLO, they attack the host country—in this case,

Jordan. Of course Jordan never asked for half a million Palestinians—the only reason they were in Jordan in the first place was because the Zionists had thrown them out of their homes in Palestine—but if you kill enough Jordanians, sooner or later, *they'll* kill the Palestinians *for* you. It's a very practical solution if you don't mind killing innocent people.

The first couple times Israel attacked Jordan, Jordan's King Hussein reacted defiantly—"*Now* we are all *fedayeen*!"—but after a few more Israeli attacks, Hussein knew that no sane leader could let his country be destroyed in a fight it had no chance of winning. (Israel has had the strongest & most modern army in the Middle East since 1947, despite its David & Goliath act.)

King Hussein had no choice: unless he was willing to watch the Israelis destroy his own country—and he knew they'd do it—he had to run the PLO out of Jordan. Morally, Hussein's job was made easier by the appearance of a PLO splinter group, the Popular Front for the Liberation of Palestine. The PFLP's cracked leader George Habash believed that Palestinians could best reach their goals by attacking Western civilians. (He must have taken the same logic class as Menachem Begin.) In September 1970 Habash's Lunatic Front for the Liberation of Palestine hijacked four Western airplanes full of tourists and forced them to land in Jordan. Habash's brutal treatment of the passengers—especially the Jewish ones—so enraged Hussein that his Army crushed the Palestinians in what became known as Black September.

A less resilient man than Arafat might have given up but not Arafat. Thousands of Palestinian commandos escaped from Jordan into Lebanon, so the resourceful Arafat rebuilt the PLO bigger and stronger than ever, in Lebanon...a fact which Lebanon would soon regret.

Israel's Dismemberment of Lebanon: Part 1

For 2,000 years, Lebanon had been the center of Middle Eastern Christianity; historically, it was usually part of Syria. After World War I, France cut off part of Syria and made it Lebanon.

From the beginning modern Lebanon was an experiment. It was the only democracy in the Middle East until the creation of Israel five years later.

It was a democracy that tried to do the impossible: It tried to be fair to the **16 different religions** of its people (while keeping its finger on the scale to tip it ever so slightly in favor of the Christians). It was a real high wire act.

They were doing great for awhile.

QUESTION: What happened? How did Lebanon go from "The Paris of the East" to The Modern Embodiment of Senseless Violence?

It Happened Little by Little

In the summer of **1948**, five years after Lebanon's birth, **130,000 Palestinians**, running for their lives to escape the Zionist terror squads, came into Lebanon. By then, Israel's Ben Gurion and his staff were already making plans to take over Southern Lebanon. Meanwhile, Palestinians,—**780,000 in the first year**—continued to flow into Lebanon, Jordan & Syria.

Lebanon survived. But things were going on in Israel that we only learned recently, through the Diaries of Israeli P. M. **Moshe Sharett**.

In **1954**, former Prime Minister **Ben Gurion** mentioned to Prime Minister **Moshe Sharett** that it would be in Israel's interest to provoke a Civil War in Lebanon between Christians and Muslims.

On **May 16, 1955** Ben Gurion got more specific: he said that Israel should provoke Lebanon's Muslims to attack Lebanon's Christians in the hope of igniting a Civil War in Lebanon. Prime Minister Sharett (whose

published Diary details this) was shocked.

Q: *So what happened?*

In 1958 America sent troops to stop the outbreak of Civil War in Lebanon. But Lebanon didn't die. It survived, recovered, and thrived. Beirut was the Middle East's major financial and intellectual center & its main connection with the West. Before Beirut was torn apart, it had as many banks as London and a currency backed by 9.4 million ounces of gold, the highest gold cover in the world. Maybe even more important was the fact that Beirut was the Middle East's center for Western journalists. By 1970, Tel Aviv had become 'the other' Middle Eastern center for journalists but Tel Aviv was an uptight little city; journalists preferred the gamy whoriness of The Paris of the East to the earnest olive drabness of Tel Aviv—the <u>Salt Lake City</u> of the East.

From the 50s to the 70s, Lebanon was a hot tourist attraction.

The Paris of the East—LIFE magazine, January 7, 1966
"The tourist boom in Lebanon has become an explosion. Last year the business swooped up another 28%, bringing some 600,000 foreign gawkers to a country which has only about two million permanent residents (more Lebanese, including Danny Thomas, live elsewhere than at home). The charm of the place is a special amalgam of the ancient Middle East with Western sophistication, a kind of Las Vegas-Riviera-St. Moritz flavored with the spices of Araby. But the traces of age hang on. Recently a scholar discovered a map of the capital city, Beirut, dating to ancient times; today's streets run precisely on the lines of the original goat paths.". . .and so on, with nine picture pages of exotic places.

1967 War

One result of the '67 Six Day Turkey Shoot was that another 500,000 Palestinians were terrorized by Israel into leaving their homes in the Occupied Territories. By 1970, half a million Palestinians—homeless, angry, impoverished, & increasingly well-armed—fled to Lebanon. Lebanon, a country of three million, was thrown into mortal turmoil.

Beirut Airport

In December 1968, the Israelis bombed **Beirut Airport**. They destroyed 13 civilian airliners belonging to **Middle East Airlines** (Lebanon's largest), at a time when Beirut was at the peak of its Paris-of-the-Eastness. As usual, Israel said it was a "retaliatory raid", but nobody fell for it. The UN Security Council condemned Israel for its brutal attack.

Even so, Lebanese tourism nosedived; Israel's tourism went up; and UP.

It was probably just a coincidence.

Destroying Lebanon

During the 70s, Palestinian attacks on Israel were always front page news in America. What we didn't hear about were the hundreds of Israeli bombings of Lebanese towns.

London Guardian correspondent Irene Beeson reported that "150 or more towns and villages in South Lebanon...have been repeatedly savaged by the Israeli armed forces since 1968."

Israel had bombed the village of Khiyam

Turning and turning in the widening gyre
The falcon cannot hear the falconer;
Things fall apart; the center cannot hold;
. . . especially when Israel lives next door.

by **W.B. Yeats** & Ron David

steadily since 1968; by the time Israel invaded south Lebanon ten years later, only 32 of Khiyam's 30,000 inhabitants remained. Ms. Beeson said, "They were massacred in cold blood".

In May 1972, **three Japanese terrorists** killed 26 people at Tel Aviv's Lydda airport. The Israelis bombed Lebanon, killing over 100 civilians.

In September 1972, when nine Israeli Olympic athletes and a trainer were killed **in Munich** by the **Black September Palestinian** group, Israel bombed Lebanon, killing over 400 civilians.

South Lebanon, Major Haddad & the SLA

The newspapers refer to South Lebanon as Israel's "Security Zone", so you might think that Israel has some legal right to be there but they don't. The Israelis have invaded South Lebanon so often that they think it's theirs.

It may as well be theirs, because since the early 60s it's been terrorized by **Major Haddad** and the thugs Israel calls **The South Lebanese Army—SLA.**

Who is Major Haddad? I referred to a 1955 meeting at which Ben Gurion suggested that Israel do its best to start a Civil War in Lebanon. **Moshe Dayan** was at the meeting. He even had a practical suggestion:

> 'Chief of Staff Dayan agreed and suggested a plan to be implemented immediately: **"Dayan favors hiring some Lebanese officer who would be ready to serve as a front man so that the Israeli Army can appear to be responding to his call to 'liberate' Christian Lebanon from the burden of its Muslim oppressors."'**
> —From the Diary of Israeli P.M. **Moshe Sharett**

Major Saad Haddad was the Lebanese officer the Israelis hired to do their dirty work. At the worst of Lebanon's Civil War, the only thing they all agreed on was that Major Haddad was the most hated

man in Lebanon. For 20 years, Major Haddad and his **South Lebanese Army** were **paid** and **armed** by **ALL** of Israel's governments to help Israel dismember Lebanon from the *inside*. Since Major Haddad had been kind enough to slaughter thousands of Lebanese and Palestinian civilians for Israel, at every opportunity Israel's grateful leaders provided him with American weapons —**especially** those deemed too brutal to use on human beings, including those adorable little 'cluster bombs'.

The Lebanese Civil War

When Lebanon's Civil War started in **April of 1975**, Christians still held power but the majority of Lebanon's population—even without the half-million Palestinians—was Muslim.

Kamal Jumblatt was a Druze Muslim who thought, rightly, that Muslims should have a larger share of the power so he decided to take that power by force. Jumblatt knew that he couldn't defeat the Christians by himself so he invited **Yasir Arafat** and the Palestinians to join him. Within a year, they had almost killed off the Lebanese Christians.

In March, 1976, an officer of the Lebanese Christian **Phalange Party** told **Sheikh Pierre Gemayel** that if they didn't get help soon, Lebanon would fall under Muslim control. Sheikh Pierre was the dignified patriarch of one of Lebanon's most powerful families. His army, the Phalange, was the toughest army in Lebanon (which isn't saying much). Sheikh Pierre asked the officer who the Christians should ask for help. The officer said, "The Israelis."

The stoic 71 year-old Sheikh Pierre could not hide his humiliation.

Israeli Prime Minister **Yitzhak Rabin** knew that the Phalange was the strongest army in Lebanon—and that they had protected Lebanon's small Jewish community for years—so

Rabin invited Sheikh Pierre and his sons, Amin and Bashir, to join talks aboard an Israeli missile boat. Sheikh Pierre could not contain his anguish: "I have been forced to turn to you, but I am filled with shame and dismay. I want to walk in Lebanon with my head held high as a Christian AND as an Arab. It is Israel's fault that the Palestinians have settled in Lebanon and taken up arms. Lebanon's tragedy is that her fate is bound up with the conflict over Palestine."

Rabin was one pissed off Prime Minister! The nerve of that old camel jockey, telling the truth to the Prime Minister of Israel!

In 1977 Kamal Jùmblatt was killed by the Syrians but the Syrians had a 30,000 man army so Jumblatt's prudent Druze warriors killed 170 local Christians. So the Christians killed some more Muslims. And so on...

LITANI—"Stone of Wisdom"

In March 1978 a PLO naval commando sneaked into Israel by boat and killed 32 Israelis. Three days later, Israel sent an army of 30,000 men, backed by armor, artillery and massive air power, into Lebanon. Israel's Army levelled entire villages in orgies of violence. In one case, **Israeli Lt. Daniel Pinto** bound four Lebanese peasants hand and foot, tortured them, strangled them to death, then tossed their bodies down a well.

Israel's poetic leaders called the massacre the "Stone of Wisdom."

A furious President Carter wrote Begin stating that unless Begin started withdrawing troops within 24 hours, Carter would cut off American funds and sponsor a United Nations resolution condemning Israel. Menachem Begin complied and turned South Lebanon over to Major Haddad.

Major Haddad showed his gratitude to Israel in his usual way: he herded 70 Lebanese Muslims into a mosque and murdered them while the Israeli Army kept out reporters. If the *true* history of Israel is ever written, Major Haddad will be named one of Israel's founding fathers.

The Dead
Israelis killed approximately 2,000 Lebanese and Palestinian civilians.
Another 250,000 were forced to flee their homes in terror.

Not one Israeli soldier was killed.
War? What war?
Israel's brave soldiers were farmers harvesting hay.

PART
8

Detours

- ◆ Peace with Egypt

- ◆ Hostages in Iran

Peace with Egypt

Sadat

Anwar Sadat was elected as Egypt's President on October 15, 1970. Sadat's first concern was to get Egypt's economy moving. One of the main drains on Egypt's economy was the need to keep a large Army ready to react in the event of a war with Israel. That seemed to be such a ridiculous waste of money that Sadat did something simple but extraordinary: he offered Israel a full Peace Treaty (Sadat's "Famous" 1971 Peace Treaty).

Israel turned him down.

Sadat wanted peace, Israel didn't; in his opinion, the only ones who could force Israel to the bargaining table were the Americans, so in July of 1972, Sadat expelled the 15,000 Soviet military advisers he'd inherited from the earlier regime, and began to make overtures to the United States to persuade/force Israel to discuss a peace treaty with Egypt. The U.S. had more important things on its mind; the only time the U.S. paid attention to the Arabs was when there was a war. (Although I'm with Sadat 100% so far, the logic of his next move seems truly bizarre.) Sadat announced that since everyone was ignoring his *peaceful* requests for peace, obviously the only way to open an international peace conference was to start a *war*, so he said he'd start a war. Nobody took him seriously.

Once the October '73 War started, the U.S. not only took him seriously, they sent Henry Kissinger over! Within a few months they'd worked out a "disengagement arrangement" for the Suez Canal and by September 1975 Egypt and Israel had signed a nonaggression pact and were on the way toward a full peace treaty.

Begin

Then, in May 1977, the famous terrorist **Menachem Begin** scored a surprising electoral victory over the **Labor** party. "**Menachem Begin**," as it is so beautifully put in *A to Z of the Middle East* by A.Gresh and D.Vidal, "**personified the touchy nationalism of his supporters.**" Begin and his boys didn't want peace, they wanted to speed up the building of Jewish settlements all over "**Eretz Israel**", beginning with the West Bank.

Sadat was not to be denied. He was going to have peace even if he had to start another war to get it! Sadat and Kissinger kept the pressure on Begin.

"Eretz Israel" translated literally, means "Biblical Israel", but in real life, depending upon what the speaker has in his mind, it can mean:

◆ modern Israel *plus* the West Bank and/or the Gaza Strip

◆ modern Israel *plus* the West Bank,Gaza and South Lebanon

◆ modern Israel *plus* the West Bank, Gaza Strip, South Lebanon, all or part of the Sinai,

◆ The most extreme version goes "from the Nile to the Euphrates," covering part of Egypt, all of Lebanon and Jordan, *plus* most or all of Syria and part of Iraq!

The frightening aspect of "Eretz Israel" is that the phrase strongly implies that the speaker thinks he is acting on orders from God! Talk about Fundamentalism!

Sadat in Jerusalem

In November 1977 Egyptian President Anwar Sadat became the first Arab head-of-state to visit Israel. One of the first things he said was, "Where is Sharon? I must meet Sharon."

When they were introduced, he said, "I tried to have you killed."

Sharon replied, "I would have done the same in your place, Anwar."

Sadat presented a peace plan to the Israeli Knesset in Jerusalem.

Camp David

Menachem Begin met with Sadat in Ismailia, Egypt, but further talks lagged. President Carter of the United States played a mediating role in September 1978, and Begin and Sadat agreed at Camp David in Maryland to negotiate a peace settlement. **On March 26, 1979**, Israel and Egypt signed a peace treaty in Washington, D.C., ending a 30-year state of war. They even drafted an ambitious document aimed at getting back the West Bank and Gaza but, although its intentions may have been good, the results weren't: the other Arab countries felt that Egypt and Israel were deciding *for* them instead of *with* them.

Finally, peace between Israel and one of its neighbors.

But the cost was high. Egypt, the most densely populated, economically powerful, militarily strong of all the Arab countries, was suddenly isolated from its peers.

Hostages in Iran

Those who would make peaceful revolution impossible will make violent revolution inevitable.

John F. Kennedy

Iran

Size: 636,296 sq.miles, slightly larger than Alaska.

Population: 45 million: Indo-European, 66%; Turk, 25%; Kurd, 5%; Semitic, Arab & others, 4%; 96% Muslim (mostly Shi'a)

Who Rules: formerly, the Shah; now the successors of Khomeini

How Created: Iran is historical Persia. At the end of WW I, Britain tried to make Iran into a protectorate. That flopped so in 1921, the Brits backed a coup led by Reza Khan, who was then made the 'Shah of Iran'.

The turning point in modern Iranian history was the two year struggle over the nationalization of Iran's oil. Nationalist groups in Iran had gained strength enough by 1951 to gain control of the Iranian Parliament and appoint Mohammad Mossadeq as Prime Minister. When he took office, Mossadeq nationalized Iran's oil. England and America resented the fact that Iran might benefit from its own oil, so—I swear—the U.S. sent the CIA to Iran to help overthrow Prime Minister Mossadeq and Iran's government. The CIA restored the Shah of Iran and his puppet government to power in August, 1953.

Revolution in Iran— When America became a superpower, we entered a world that had been shaped by European superpowers—mainly Britain and France—to *their* great advantage, and to the *disadvantage* of the countries they colonized or used in other ways. They redrew the boundaries of ancient countries and helped overthrow people-based governments and backed goons that they could "do business with." That was especially true in places with oil like Iran.

Sometimes America really does stand by its principles and support governments

of the people—but sometimes greed wins out over principle like it did in Iran. American corporations liked the Shah of Iran because he was a guy you could do business with and he hated communism (probably because they didn't pay as well as our guys did).

The Shah was good for business and bad for the people of Iran. He brutally suppressed anyone who opposed him, he was out of touch with his own people, and just before the revolution, he closed down nearly 250,000 small businesses.

(And if that isn't bad enough, he was buddies with Richard Nixon.)

So in February 1979, when a revolution led by the Iyatollah Khomeini ended the Shah's 37-year reign, it wasn't just some Muslim fanatics who wanted the Shah out of there, it was most of the people of Iran.

I am not a great fan of Khomeini—as far as I'm concerned, you can take *all* of those fire-breathing holy men (and that includes Menachem Begin *and* Moses) and drop them off in my old neighborhood in Detroit—but the Shah, often with the U.S.'s help, repressed/destroyed/killed off all the secular, sane, reasonable alternatives. You have to be a little bit crazy to stand up to *that* much power. That old fire-breathing dragon Khomeini was the only one left with the stones to do it!

The Hostage Crisis

November 4, 1979, exactly one year after the Shah's forces had shot student demonstrators, Iranian students occupied the American Embassy in Tehran and held 61 Americans hostage. The students were furious because the Shah was permitted to enter the United States—even if it was for medical treatment. If America had *any* credibility left with Iran, we lost it when the students discovered documents in our Embassy revealing that the CIA had been interfering in Iran's internal affairs.

Two weeks after the siege, the students released the black and female hostages. They kept the other 52. A few months later America tried a flashy rescue like the Israelis had pulled off with such panache at Entebbe but it was a disaster. (One of the helicopters crashed into a transport plane.) Eight people died.

Carter should have hired the Israelis. (Or sent the Shah back.)

If the Shah of Iran had any sense of honor, he would have voluntarily gone back to Iran. Instead, the inconsiderate jerk died before the hostages were released. The hostages were held for 444 days until January 21, 1981, when Jimmy Carter walked out and Ronald Reagan walked in.

(There's an interesting charge that keeps popping up. They call it "October Surprise." I suspect it's true but I'm not convinced by the evidence; if I said any more about it, I'd just be spreading rumors.)

1979: July 16—**General Saddam Hussein** is named President of Iraq

1980: September—Saddam Hussein attacks Iran; the Iran/Iraq war begins
(...But don't be too quick to pass judgement.)

1981: June 7—Israeli warplanes destroy an Iraqui nuclear plant.
The United States, the Soviet Union, and other countries , including France (which sold the nuclear reactor to Iraq), condemn the raid. Menachem Begin gives a news conference saying that he was preventing another Holocaust (He's new at his job; he hasn't quite gotten the hang of International Law yet. Maybe in a century or two.)

1981: June 19—The UN Security Council condemns Israel's raid.
Israel, as usual, acting on orders straight from God, ignores the United Nations, the U.S. and every civilized country in the world.

The "Two Week War"

'82:

Israel Destroys Lebanon

Every politician in Israel knows that voters respond affectionately to violence against the PLO so, on July 17, 1981, during Menachem Begin's shaky campaign for reelection, Israel bombed "PLO strongholds" in Lebanon. (America may have Smart Bombs, but only Israel has Tautology Bombs—no matter what they hit, it's a "PLO stronghold.") The savvy Arafat, aware that Begin's reelection campaign was underway, didn't retaliate. After five days of heavy Israeli bombing, Arafat figured he'd con his more radical constituents (*without* risking Israeli pre-election wrath) by shooting a few shells into the uninhabited desert.

That was all the excuse Begin needed: Israel bombed the felafel out of PLO headquarters in Beirut.

Arafat, forced to fight back, shelled Kiryat Shmonah in Northern Israel. Five Israelis—and nearly five-<u>hundred</u> Lebanese and Palestinians were killed.

The humorous Arafat (the guy should be a stand-up-comic) bragged about his "great victory" in the **"Two Week War."**

Begin was so depressed that he signed a truce with the PLO.

*Shame.*To sign a truce with the PLO was to acknowledge its existence.

Menachem Begin never forgave Arafat for making him sign that truce. During a visit to the United States, late in 1981, Begin told an Israeli general who visited him at the Waldorf Astoria Hotel, "I want Arafat in his bunker!"

The PLO Keeps the Truce

In Begin's softening mind, Yasir Arafat had become Adolph Hitler.

In August 1981 Begin appointed Ariel Sharon Israeli Minister of Defense.

The justification for Israel's long-standing refusal to sign a truce with the PLO was, 'Why sign a truce when we know those animals won't honor it?' You will, therefore, understand why, in Begin's view, the PLO had done something infinitely worse than making him SIGN that bloody truce: those underhanded heathens were actually HONORING it!

So, in the Spring of 1982 (nine months had passed), although the PLO had <u>not</u> broken the truce, Israel complained of PLO attacks.

The United States asked for proof.

The Israelis produced a list of 32 violations.

The Americans pointed out that every one of those violations had occurred in Lebanon where Israeli soldiers had no legal right to be.

Arafat, smelling that Israel was looking for any jive excuse to break the truce and eradicate the PLO, contacted Washington. The Americans assured Arafat that as long as he kept the ceasefire, Israel would not attack the PLO.

Israel Breaks the Truce

On June 6, Israel invaded Lebanon

Yasir Arafat was in Saudi Arabia when he got news of Israel's attack.

(Arafat has never been given sufficient credit for his sense of humor.)

When he learned of Israel's invasion, Arafat said, "We'll teach the Israelis a lesson, as we have in the past."

On **June 7**, Philip Habib, President Reagan's special envoy to the Middle East, met with Prime Minister Begin.

Begin gave Habib his word that Israel would not attack the Syrians.

The next day Habib was in Damascus assuring Syrian President Assad that he had Begin's sworn word that Israel would not attack any Syrian bases when they both learned that, at 2:00 that afternoon, the Israeli air force had <u>already</u> attacked the Syrian missile batteries in the Bekka Valley!

Reagan was furious. He demanded that Israel agree to a ceasefire. Prime Minister Begin refused.

Israel continued its massive invasion of Lebanon.

SIDON—Bulldozing the Casbah

Israeli General Yitzhak Mordechai knew that, six years earlier, even the roughneck Syrians were stalled when they tried to enter the crowded streets of the Casbah—the 4,000 year-old center of the ancient Lebanese city of Sidon—so General Mordechai sent in bulldozers to widen the streets so that IDF tanks could maneuver easily. The Israelis levelled half of the buildings in the ancient city. The Israelis were not only destroying the country and people of Lebanon, they were destroying its <u>history</u>

General Mordechai took the city in three days with no Israeli casualties.

Ein Hilweh— "Victory or Death!"

The Israelis surrounded *Ein Hilweh*, a Palestinian refugee camp outside Sidon. The Israelis sent the message, "Whoever does not bear arms will not be harmed," but the Palestinians weren't having any more of that bull.

They screamed, "Victory or death!"

General Mordechai flew in a team of Israeli psychologists to advise him on how to deal with such irrational behavior. As usual, the shrinks didn't suggest anything that worked in the real world so, once again, General Mordechai sent in the tanks.

Note: All of this factual information was taken from *Israel's Lebanon War* by **Ze'ev Schiff & Ehud Ya'ari,** considered the definitive account of Israel's '82 invasion of Lebanon. **Schiff** is Military Correspondent for Israel's largest newspaper; **Ya'ari** is Middle East correspondent for Israel TV. As bad as it makes Israel look, the Israelis censored 20-50% of the original manuscript—so they're probably 35% *worse* than they look here!

On **Thursday, June 11**, America's Habib negotiated a ceasefire between Israel and the Syrians. On the next day the Syrians had their guard down because of the ceasefire so Israel attacked the Syrian 85th Brigade.

On **Sunday, June 13**, over Israeli state radio, Prime Minister Begin solemnly swore that Israel had no intention of invading Beirut. Begin's denial was immediately followed by a live report from Beirut describing Israeli tanks ALREADY IN the Lebanese capital!

Philip Habib, under no further illusions as to Israel's trustworthiness, warned Arafat, "If an agreement is not reached quickly, the Israelis will break into West Beirut."

Can you imagine what Arafat did?

The wily bugger discovered a quote from the Bible prophesying Israel's defeat and he had it distributed among Israeli soldiers:

"The violence done to Lebanon will destroy you." Habakkuk 2:17

Hitler in Beirut...?

By the beginning of August the Israelis had destroyed most of Beirut.

Prime Minister Begin was so excited that he sent a note to President Reagan: "I feel as though I have sent an army to Berlin to wipe out Hitler in the bunker."

President Reagan, despite the fact that he himself had acted bravely in several World War II movies, apparently thought that there was enough difference between Berlin and Beirut to demand that Israel return to the lines they had reached on August 1.

The Israelis ignored him.

Philip Habib worked feverishly toward a peace plan in which Arafat and the PLO could leave Lebanon alive; the Israelis worked even more feverishly on slaughtering the Palestinians before any agreement could be reached:

On Monday, August 9, Israel hit Beirut with 36 bombing missions.

Tuesday, there were 16.

On Thursday, August 18, Israel hit Beirut with 72 bombing missions.

President Reagan (who isn't exactly a dove) called Israel's bombing of Beirut "unfathomable and senseless" and coerced Israel into a truce.

PLO Leaves Beirut

One week later, the first PLO evacuees left Beirut by ship. By then, the United States trusted Israel so little that American warships escorted the Palestinians out of Beirut's harbor.

Ariel Sharon, all belly and bluster, bragged that Israel had the 4th-strongest army in the world. I'm sure they did.

Israel's Lebanon War, by Ze'ev Schiff and Ehud Ya'ari presents incontrovertible evidence that:

♦ In 1981 the PLO signed a truce with Israel.

♦ The truce held for a year until <u>Israel</u> broke it and invaded Lebanon.

♦ Israel's invasion of Lebanon

was an act of unmitigated aggression.

◆ The 4th strongest army in the world destroyed Rashidiyeh refugee camp, killing hundreds of Palestinians, used 'anti-personnel' bombs on the trapped residents of Ein Hilweih refugee camp, coldly murdering hundreds more Palestinians, besieged Beirut, cutting off food, water and medical supplies and then, when the residents were nicely trapped, **dropped cluster bombs and phosphorous bombs on schools, orphanages and hospitals.**

The Sabra & Shatila Massacres

On **August 23**, two days after the PLO began its departure from Lebanon, **Bashir Gemayel**, Sheik Pierre's son, was elected President of Lebanon. Within a week of Bashir's election, Menachem Begin summoned Bashir to Israel, and bullied and insulted him. . .but worst of all, Begin had tried to make Beshir shake the hand of the despised **Major Haddad,** who Begin "suggested" should be Lebanon's next Minister of Defense. Finally, the slippery Bashir found something he couldn't just grin and lie his way through. He would never shake that man's hand. It may have been the only honorable thing Bashir ever did in his life.

Two weeks later, on the afternoon of **September 14**, Bashir was killed.

To cut to the heart of it, the Israeli Army surrounded **Shatila & Sabra** refugee camps, met with Bashir's revenge-bent **Phalangist** army—Sharon said, **"I don't want a single one of them left."**—let the Phalangists into the camps, told the

Knesset (Israel's `House of Representatives') in the kind of double-meaning language that drug-sellers use, and everyone went away, winking and nodding about what was going on without saying anything you could use in court.

Except for Sharon and good old General Eitan. It was just another day in Paradise for them.

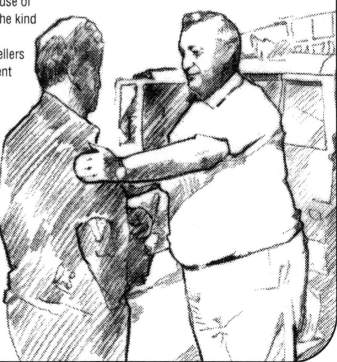

There's Something I Don't Understand

After the massacres at Sabra & Shatila, 400,000 conscience-stricken Israelis protested in Tel Aviv (and thousands more in America) because Israel had **INdirectly** allowed the Phalangists to murder **800** Palestinians.

Yet when Israel **DIRECTLY** kills 30,000 people, they don't mourn?

Why would Jewish anguish focus on Sabra & Shatila, the crime they **tolerated** instead of the crime they **perpetrated?**

There is only one plausible reason why the Jewish people focused on the Sabra & Shatila massacre. That was the only way to focus the world's attention on the only part of the crime they *DIDN'T* commit, **to cover the enormous crime they DID commit.**

The Dead
In the Shatila & Sabra camps about
800 Palestinians

The Dead
In the First 3 Months of Israel's Invasion of Lebanon
19,085 Lebanese & Palestinians
...84% were civilians...

The Dead
By the End of Israel's Invasion of Lebanon about *500* Israelis
and
30,000—50,000
Lebanese & Palestinians

The Longest War

Jacobo Timerman had been imprisoned and tortured in Argentina because he spoke his conscience and because he was a Zionist Jew. He came to Israel in 1979 to escape oppression and to be, for once in his life, happy. What he found in Israel did not make him happy. T*he Longest War* was Jacobo Timerman's anguished description of Israel's invasion of Lebanon.

". . .since we passed the border into Lebanon I have not seen a single house that did not show some war damage. . ."

". . . Israel had attacked a neighboring country without being attacked. . ."

". . . Israel brought destruction to entire cities: Tyre, Sidon, Damur, Beirut."

". . .trying only to imagine how the dead were killed. . ."

"This is what I try to do in Tyre and Sidon as I gaze on these ancient cities, reduced to ruins in a couple of weeks."

Why?

According to Jacobo Timerman, on <u>one day</u>, Sunday, June 13, doctors at the American University in Beirut removed 1,100 limbs from victims of Israel's bombing of Beirut.

On June 4 Israel bombed a children's hospital in the Sabra refugee camp.

On June 12 Israel shelled an Armenian sanitarium near Beirut.

<u>And</u> the Gaza hospital in Beirut.

<u>And</u> the Acre Hospital in Beirut.

<u>And</u> a hospital in Aley.

On June 24 Israel bombed the Islamic Home for Invalids.

An American nurse working in Beirut testifed that Israel "dropped bombs on everything, including hospitals, orphanages and...a school bus carrying 35 young schoolgirls".

By August 4, there was only <u>one</u> orphanage left standing in Beirut. Israel had destroyed the other eight.

On <u>one day</u>, the Israelis shelled 17 different hospitals.

In <u>one month</u>, more children were killed in Beirut by Israelis than during 30 years of terrorism in Israel.

Who are the people who do these things?

Surely, they can't be Jews.

And Israel smote him with the
edge of the sword and
possessed his land.
Numbers 21:24

Señor, señor, do you know where
we're headin'?
Lincoln Country Road or
Armageddon?
Bob Dylan—"Señor (Tale of
Yankee Power)"

It's an opinion but it seems so obvious that maybe it'll become a fact.
I think that Jews on either side of the 20th century, from every corner of the world, have

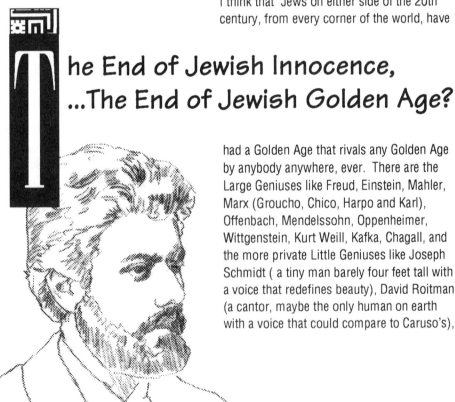

The End of Jewish Innocence, ...The End of Jewish Golden Age?

had a Golden Age that rivals any Golden Age by anybody anywhere, ever. There are the Large Geniuses like Freud, Einstein, Mahler, Marx (Groucho, Chico, Harpo and Karl), Offenbach, Mendelssohn, Oppenheimer, Wittgenstein, Kurt Weill, Kafka, Chagall, and the more private Little Geniuses like Joseph Schmidt (a tiny man barely four feet tall with a voice that redefines beauty), David Roitman (a cantor, maybe the only human on earth with a voice that could compare to Caruso's),

Philip Roth, Woody Allen, Sontag, Mailer, Bellow, Arthur Miller, Bob Dylan, Lenny Bruce, Allen Ginzberg, and people who *lived* in a way that you could respect and learn from, like Schwerner and Goodman, the civil rights workers who were killed in Mississippi and Daniel Ellsberg, and my ruthlessly moral friend, Stewart Justman.

If I were to choose the ones that move me most at this time in my life, I would probably say Grace Paley, Noam Chomsky, Josef Schmidt, David Roitman, and Mahler. The writer that moved me most strongly was Malamud but I think his writing died a few years before he did. I have an odd theory: Israel is killing Jewish genius.

The innocence is gone.

Maybe we'll talk more about that later.

> "According to figures provided by Minister of the Interior Yosef Burg, in 1980 ten Jews were killed by terrorists and in 1981, eight. In contrast, we have killed about a thousand terrorists in 1982, and caused the loss of life of thousands of inhabitants of an enemy country. So it results that for every 6-8 Jews sacrificed, we kill in return thousands of Gentiles. This is, undoubtedly, a spectacular situation, an uncommon success of Zionism."
> Migvan (Labor Party), Oct/Nov 1982, quoting Aluf Hareven of the Van Leer Institute, in a debate on "Zionism -82" held at Tel Aviv University

CHAPTER 40

Terrorism—1: the Middle East

If you actually *read* the quote above, two things probably surprised you:

◆ How few Jews were killed.

◆ And how many "terrorists" were killed.

["Terrorist" means, in descending order, Palestinian, Arab, whoever the Tautology Bomb hit. On rare occasions, it means *terrorist*.]

(We'll pretend we didn't notice the somewhat bloodthirsty tone of the speaker, and the use of the word "Gentile.")

Money-Back Guarantee

I said it earlier and I'll say it again: In *every* encounter between Jews and Arabs—I mean "terrorists"—there'll be at least ten dead Arabs for every Jew.

THE PALESTINIANS
Long, Bloody Search
For Nationhood

What Exactly is Terrorism?

Israeli Ambassador Benjamin Netanyahu compiled and edited a book of essays on terrorism a few years ago that won the heart of Ronald Reagan when President Rambo was in his "Make-my-day" phase. Netanyahu's book was racist slander—he said the same thing about Muslims that Nazis and other heavy-duty antiSemites said about Jews—but he did have a good definition of Terrorism:

Terrorism is the deliberate and systematic murder, maiming, and menacing of the innocent to inspire fear for political purposes.

That, to me is a perfect definition of Terrorism.

It fits Israel's **Land Clearing Operations** to a tee. The Zionists "deliberately and systematically murdered, maimed and menaced the innocent for political purposes," until 780,000 Palestinians ran for their lives. The "political purpose", obviously, was to take down the 2,000-year-old sign that said **Palestine** and replace it with one that said **Israel.**

Pioneers of Terrorism

Israeli historian Simha Flapan (in his book *Zionism and the Palestinians*) says that Zionist terror groups "established the pattern of terrorism adopted 30 years later by Al-Fatah."

- ◆ Jewish terrorists killed 338 British citizens in Palestine during the 40s
- ◆ Jewish terrorists assassinated at least 40 Jews during the pre-State period
- ◆ Jewish terrorists blew up American installations & blamed Egyptians
- ◆ In December 1954, the Israeli air force hijacked a Syrian airliner to get hostages to exchange for Israeli soldiers? That was **20 years** before the PLO did it! The PLO didn't start the hijackings—Israel did!
  The Israelis don't take enough credit for their creativity.
- ◆ Jewish terrorists invented the letter bomb! (Where would mankind be without the Uzi?)

A Partial List of [mostly Arab] Terrorists

1968— Two Arabs attack an Israeli
airliner in Athens airport, killing
one
1972— Ten Israelis are murdered during
the Olymic games in Munich
1974— Ma'alot massacre—
Palestinians kill 22 Israeli children
(My God)
1976— Israelis hijack Lebanese Muslim boats & give them to
Major Haddad
1976— Israelis rescue 110 hostages held at Uganda's Entebbe Airport
1984— A CIA-sponsored car bomb kills 80 people in West Beirut
1985— 3 Israelis killed in Cyprus
70 Tunisians & Palestinians killed in Tunis by Israel
One death in Achille Lauro hijacking
60 deaths in Israel's hijacking of Egyptian airliner.
Terrorist attacks at Vienna and Rome airports kill 18 people
Israelis kill two CBS cameramen
1986— Israelis hijack a Libyan airliner

I Hate ALL of Them!

But lets get a few things straight:
- There are more Experts on Terrorism than there are Terrorists
- More Americans die in their bathtubs than are killed by terrorists in a year
- There was no such thing as the PLO until Israel stole Palestine
- There was no such thing as Fatah or PFLP until Israel stole Palestine
- There was no such thing as an Arab Terrorist until Israel stole Palestine
- No Arab *ever* went to Kiev or Warsaw or Brooklyn to terrorize Jews or steal Jewish land
- Arabs believed in America's promise of Democracy & Self-Determination until we proved by our actions that we didn't believe in Democracy *for them*

We should take them at their word and give them a chance.

Speaking of Terrorists

In 1983, Menachem Begin, the terrorist who led the Deir Yassin massacre and the bombing of the King David Hotel, resigned as Prime Minister of Israel only to be replaced by Yitzhak Shamir, the Stern Gang terrorist leader who ordered the murder of the UN Mediator Bernadotte. If we don't deal with terrorists, why do we deal with *them*?

Khadaffi's Daughter

On April 5 a bomb exploded in a Berlin disco, killing an American soldier & a Turkish woman. Ronald Reagan blamed Libya. President Reagan said he had "irrefutable evidence" that Khadaffi was responsible for the disco attack.

April 14: America bombs Libya.

◆ A residential neighborhood in Tripoli [Libya] was demolished
◆ Most Western nations condemned the bombing
◆ All Arab countries condemned the bombing
◆ France refused to let American planes fly over its air space
◆ The Russian ambassador cancelled a trip to America in protest
◆ **Khadaffi's infant daughter was killed in the bombing**
◆ **And President Reagan's "irrefutable evidence" turns out to be phony.**

I'm sorry, Khadaffi.

Portrait of a Terrorist

On October 28, 1938 the Germans launched an assault against Polish Jews. They snatched children from the streets and jammed them, along with thousands of others, including the aged and infirm, into trucks and trains bound for the Polish border.

Among this mass of human misery was the Grynszpan family. One of the sons, 17-year-old Herschel, who had fled to Paris, read over and over again a letter from his father describing the family's suffering. The boy, who had been overwrought since he left Poland, bought a pistol and went to the German embassy. He asked to see the German Ambassador but instead they gave him a flunkie, Ernst vom Rath— so Herschel shot the flunkie. On November 9 vom Rath, who was one of the few

Nazis sympathetic to Jews, died of his wounds. At two o'clock the next morning a wave of arson, looting, murder and arrest began and Herschel Grynszpan, in the custody of French police, broke down and cried, "Being a Jew is not a crime. I am not a dog. I have a right to live and the Jewish people have a right to exist on this earth. Wherever I have been I have been chased like an animal."

Condensed from WHILE SIX MILLION DIED by Arthur D. Morse
Chapter 12: The Night of Broken Glass

"Being a Palestinian is not a crime. I am not a dog. I have a right to live and the Palestinian people have a right to exist on this earth. Wherever I have been I have been chased like an animal."

Let's stop kidding ourselves. Terrorists aren't born, they're *made*.

There's even a formula for making them:

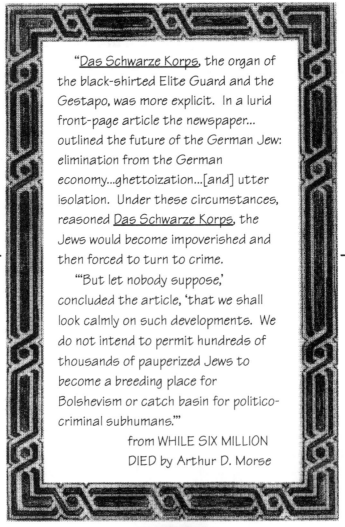

"Das Schwarze Korps, the organ of the black-shirted Elite Guard and the Gestapo, was more explicit. In a lurid front-page article the newspaper... outlined the future of the German Jew: elimination from the German economy...ghettoization...[and] utter isolation. Under these circumstances, reasoned Das Schwarze Korps, the Jews would become impoverished and then forced to turn to crime.

"'But let nobody suppose,' concluded the article, 'that we shall look calmly on such developments. We do not intend to permit hundreds of thousands of pauperized Jews to become a breeding place for Bolshevism or catch basin for politico-criminal subhumans.'"

from WHILE SIX MILLION DIED by Arthur D. Morse

The Intifada

> When you have robbed a man of everything, he is no longer in your power. He is free again.
>
> Aleksandr Solzenhitsyn

In 1967 when Israel first took the Territories, the Palestinians kept the faith. They knew about the UN's 'inviolable' law of the "inadmissibility of the acquisition of territory by war", so they had expected the world community to make the Israelis leave. Instead, the Occupation had lasted 20 years, during which time the Israelis built illegal settlements over most of the Territories, took away most of the Palestinian men between 16 and 60, and brutalized whoever was left.

By the mid 1980s the people in the Territories had been abandoned by the other Arab countries and demonized by America—Kissinger had made a secret deal with Israel not to talk to the PLO, and America's UN Ambassador Andrew Young had been forced to resign for merely *talking* to the PLO.

The PLO, for years the people in the Territories' only source of hope, had been run out of Lebanon, virtually abandoned violence and made peace offer after peace offer that was *not only rejected*, but was *written out of history* the day after it was made. (We will talk about that in the chapter on Peace.)

Worst of all, the Palestinians living *inside* the Occupied Territories had begun to feel isolated from Palestinians living outside the Territories.

The Israeli abuses, especially the constant humiliation, kept getting worse.

By the end of 1987 the people in the Territories knew that there was no help coming from anywhere. They were alone.

December 8, 1987— An Israeli Army truck killed four Palestinians in the Gaza Strip.
December 9, 1987— The next day, the Gaza Strip Palestinians found themselves standing in front of the Israeli soldiers, confronting the soldiers with rocks in response to, or in honor of, their four dead Arab brothers.

The Israelis killed one Palestinian, mortally wounded another, and wounded 15.

The unrest spread quickly to the West Bank. Israeli efforts to suppress protests in the Occupied Territories failed, as the sudden explosion of Palestinian anger turned into a sustained uprising. By Dec. 18, Israeli soldiers had killed 17 Palestinians.

December 22, 1987— The United Nations Security Council (the United States abstained from the vote) unanimously approves a resolution that "strongly deplores" Israel's brutal handling of the Palestinian protests.

December 25, 1987— Israel announces that it has incarcerated nearly a thousand Palestinian protesters.

January 3, 1988— Israel announces that it will deport 9 Palestinians. The U.S. and the other members of the UN Security Council unanimously call on Israel to halt the deportations. Israel deports 4 of the 9 Palestinians.

January 19, 1988— 38 Palestinians had been shot to death during the first six weeks of the Intifada. Israel's brutality is criticized by America & England; 30,000 Israeli demonstrators march on TelAviv to protest the policy.

February 15, 1988— Israeli soldiers buried four Palestinians alive in the West Bank. After the soldiers left, the Arab residents uncovered the buried protesters. All four were injured but survived.

March 10, 1988— Palestinian leaders issue leaflets asking all Arab police in the Occupied Territories to resign; nearly half of the 1,000 police resign.

March 28, 1988— In response to the worldwide outrage at their treatment of the Intifada Palestinians, Israel announces that it .will seal off the Occupied Territories. Journalists will not be allowed in without a military escort.

No Witness, no Crime. . ?

The Dead—1989—

The U.S. State Department's human rights report criticizes Israel for using gunfire against Palestinian protesters. Since the Intifada began, 85 Israelis and about 900 Palestinians had been killed.

Ten to one.

America Goes to the Middle East

- ◆ TWO STYLES OF CENSORSHIP—in Iran & America
- ◆ THE TWO GULF WARS—the One in America & the One in Iraq
- ◆ The PROPAGANDA War: Arab-Bashing in America
- ◆ Doin 'the Madrid Dozens' & Shopping for Real Estate, Israeli Style
- ◆ MONEY [<u>American</u> MONEY]
- ◆ The World Trade Center BOMBING & The Mother of ALL Propaganda Wars

Lord, make me chaste—but not yet.
St. Augustine

Two Styles of Censorship— In Iran They Kill You... In America They..?

"Not the violent conflict between parts of the truth, but the quiet suppression of half of it, is the formidable evil. There is always hope when people are forced to listen to both sides."
—John Stuart Mill

Righteous Indigestion

In February 1989 the **Iyatollah Khomeini** called on Muslims everywhere to kill author **Salman Rushdie** for writing *The Satanic Verses*. Rushdie, stunned, rushed into hiding. Bookstores got phone calls warning them not to display *The Satanic Verses,* booksellers were paralyzed between greed and fear, and writers no one had seen in years came out of hibernation to protest. Norman Mailer, Susan Sontag, E.L. Doctorow and other of the most famous writers in New York turned out to scream down Khomeini and the bookstores that wouldn't risk their lives for books. Norman Mailer, bless his little heart, was so outraged that he offered not only his own life but the life of every writer. Puff puff.

Taking a Stand Against the Penguin

It costs a writer, living in the comfort of America, nothing to puff out his chest against Khomeni.
Taking a stand against Khomeini is like taking a stand against Professor Moriarty or The Penguin.

Worst of all, there is a <u>real</u> censorship problem right here in America that Mailer and other writers with clout could do some <u>real</u> good in opposing—if they had the nerve. And I think they don't.

American censorship is more subtle. As John Stuart Mill said, "There is always hope when people are forced to listen to both sides."

EXAMPLE: In 1985 a three-part PBS TV program, "Flashpoint—Israel & the Palestinians", was cancelled in New York; the censors swore on a stack of bagels that the cancellation had nothing to do with the fact that one show presented the Palestinian viewpoint. When they finally aired the program, they showed only the two pro-Israeli films. They eventually showed the *almost* fair-to-the-Palestinians show but *insisted* that a panel of Israelites "explain" to you what you thought you just saw. *Then*, the poor lady who made the film had to keep apologizing for *accepting* Arab money to make the film! (I swear, Mom, I *don't* do it with pigs!) Jewish money is cool. Arab money comes straight from the Devil!

EXAMPLE: The Palestinian scholar **Edward Said,** was asked by a major New York publisher to recommend some Third World novels. Edward Said suggested an Arab writer named **Naguib Mahfouz**. The embarrassed publisher weaseled out of the offer with the lame explanation **"Arabic after all is a controversial language."** Naguib Mahfouz won the Nobel Prize for literature in 1988 so the racist publisher lost out.

EXAMPLE: Paul Findley was a Senator who, following his conscience, decided on a few occasions to be *mildly* critical of Israel. AIPAC (the Israeli "lobby"—featured in the Chapter on *Money*) tried to bully him but he didn't go for it, so AIPAC put a lot of money into Findley's opponent and spread dirty rumors about Findley. After Findley lost the election he decided to do some research on censorship of Americans who were critical of Israel.

When he finished the book—which was filled with documented cases of critics of Israel being censored, intimidated and harrassed—Findley was told, *surprise!*—that he'd never find a publisher for a subject that "sensitive." It took him years but he did find a publisher. But try to find a copy of his book.

EXAMPLE: "American correspondents in Beirut report privately that the New York office of a major television network suppressed a 1975 documentary on Israeli military actions in southern Lebanon." [Noam Chomsky, *The Fateful Triangle,* p191]

EXAMPLE: A few years ago I wanted to check out the story of two CBS cameramen killed in Lebanon by the Israeli Army so I called CBS. A low level person took my number and gave it to his boss; the boss called and said no CBS cameramen were *ever* killed in Lebanon. He said I must have been thinking of an NBC cameraman killed in Bangkok. I tried NBC. After a few more detours I called CBS again, got the same low level person, asked *half* of a question but he/she stopped me—
"He knows."

I said, "Knows <u>what</u>?" *"He knows what you're looking for."* I was so excited I felt like I was breaking the Watergate scam. "What do I do now?" I asked. The person said, *"I'm not saying another word. Ask him. Keep asking. He knows."*

The boss came to the phone, a real smoothie, kept telling me I had the wrong network or the wrong something, then, after ten minutes or so of my nagging, *BAM*, like Gregory Peck coming out of amnesia, he suddenly remembers exactly what I'm talking about, says he'll copy the entire file and send it to me for nothing.

A week later I received a file of 40 articles; 39 of them were evasive; the 40th one by **Alexander Cockburn**, from *The Wall Street Journal*, Thurs, Apr 11, 1985:

On March 11, 1985, Israeli tanks rolled into the Lebanese town of Zrariya and killed 35 men, women and children. Reporters tried to talk to the survivors, the survivors said the Israelis told them that if journalists or TV crews were allowed into their town, the Israelis would destroy every house in the village.

On March 21, NBC cameraman **Tewfik Ghazawi** and soundman **Bahij Metni**, both Lebanese employees of CBS, were killed by an Israeli tank shell in the Lebanese village of Kfar Melki. **Ayyad Harakeh**, their driver, lost both legs. **Edward Joyce**, President of CBS news, was so furious he publicly accused the Israelis of **murder**. CBS sent News VP Ernest Leiser to Israel. A week later Leiser came back cowed like a puppy and reported the lies the Israelis told him. Each time one lie was exposed, they'd come up with a new one!

Alexander Cockburn, who is nobody's fool, proves beyond a doubt that the Israelis killed the men intentionally. He goes through the type of tank, the magnification power of the scope, the distance from the tank to the TV team—it's idiot-proof; no question about it.

TV stations and major publishers who suppress anything critical of Israel—*and* won't let us hear the Arabs' side of the story? Plus a TV network that's so protective of Israel that they let the Israelis kill their employees, *then help them cover it up?*

What's going on? It can't be as obvious as it seems?

Saddam WHO?

Saddam Hussein is now so recognizable in America that any day now I expect to see him doing a Pepsi commercial, but when he first came on the scene, not many Americans knew who he was. Or what part he played in America's past.

Suckering the Kurds

In 1972 the Shah of Iran asked for America's help in slowly ruining Iraq (they call it 'destabilizing'). President Nixon, who was already severely 'tilted' toward Iran, mailed Henry Kissinger to Iran. Kissinger and the Shah decided on the sickening plan of destabilizing Iraq by *supporting the* **Kurds** *just enough to keep them fighting but not enough for the Kurds to win.* The Kurds thought the US was helping them but we were just using them to sap Iraq's resources, using one Iraqui to kill another.

In 1975 the Shah and Saddam Hussein (Iraq's #2 man) signed a treaty; nobody needed the Kurds any more, so the US cut off all aid, leaving the Kurds to Saddam.

In 1976 George Bush became director of the CIA and carried on a mutually beneficial relationship with Saddam Hussein, an excellent killer and torturer.

In 1979 Saddam Hussein became President of Iraq. Also in 1979, the Iyatollah Khomeini took over Iran, and America (to say the least) 'tilted' away from Iran. So, in 1980, when Saddam Hussein attacked Iran, it was perfectly reasonable to assume that the US "actively encouraged" Saddam Hussein to attack Iran.

CHAPTER

43

The Two Gulf Wars—
the War in America & the War in Iraq

That Sounds Like a Weird Foreign Policy

Thanks mainly to Henry Kissinger, since 1972 our foreign policy has been playing one side against the other. We back Iran, then Iraq, then both at the same time. It's a high-profit version of what Kissinger did to the Kurds: keep them fighting and make billions of dollars selling weapons to both sides. If peace breaks out, send in the CIA to start up a new war. Our slimy but profitable foreign policy was kept secret from the American people but thugs like Saddam Hussein knew it very well.

August 25, 1988—	Iraq gasses Kurds near the Turkish border
October 2, 1989—	President Bush signs National Security Directive 26, calling for closer US ties to Iraq.
October 31, 1989—	Baker calls Yeuter to urge him to approve additional loan guarantees for Iraq.
January 1990—	Investigations discover $3 billion in unauthorized BNL loans to Iraq.
January 17, 1990—	Bush waives the embargo placed by Congress on Eximbank credits to Iraq.

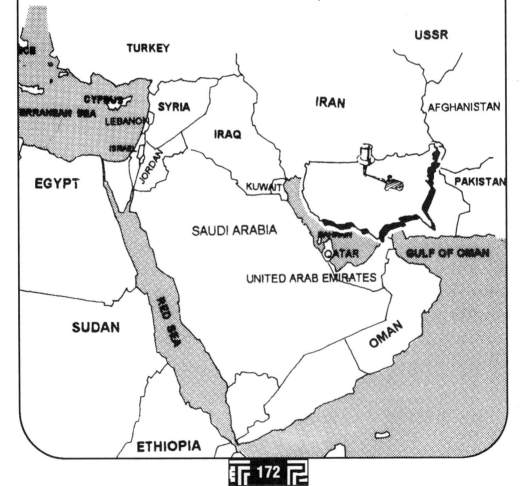

Saddam Hussein had been one of George Bush's pet alligators for 14 years so he had every right to be surprised when Bush started calling him Hitler, selfrighteously proclaiming, "This aggression cannot stand," and especially when President Bush sent thousands of American soldiers into the desert with large American guns.

I'm getting a little ahead of myself.

April Fool

On August 2, 1990, the Iraqui army entered Kuwait. A couple days earlier, Saddam Hussein conferred with April Glaspie, America's Ambassador to Iraq and told her in that same kind of drug seller talk the Israeli Knesset used on the night of the Sabra & Shatila massacre, that he was going to drop by Kuwait, and she signaled him back that it was cool with her.

When she came back to the US her bosses changed their minds so she changed hers. Saddam, who knows a thing or two about survival, had secretly taped their conversation, so when she denied that it had ever taken place, Slick Saddam sent a copy of the tape to **The Mother of all Newspapers,** *The NY Times*. Ms. Glaspie was embarrassed but our government carried on like Saddam's tape didn't exist.

Amazingly, so did our media. TV news reports almost never mentioned it—and none of the *regular* people I know had ever heard of it!

False Advertising

What set a lot of people off *against* Saddam Hussein and *for* Kuwait was an emotional pitch by a lady about Iraqi soldiers ripping babies out of incubators and smashing their heads against the wall. It was revealed after the war—it was even in the *TV Guide*—that this lady was a Kuwaiti movie actress (she may also have been the Kuwaiti Ambassador's daughter!) but they got away with it. The entire scam was put together by an Advertising Agency.

The best estimate of the number of people Saddam killed in Kuwait is about 3,000.

> **Sept 6,1990—** President Bush sends 125,000 US soldiers to Saudi Arabia
> **Sept 17,1990—** Air Force Chief of Staff Dugan is fired for saying that Israelis said "best way to hurt Saddam was by targeting him, his family, his mistress..."

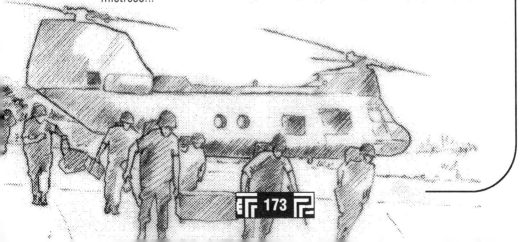

What was to Negotiate?—
Saddam was Either IN Kuwait or OUT

Some people said "Let's negotiate", others refused, saying "What's to negotiate?" Several countries (including Iraq) made proposals for getting Saddam out of Kuwait without a war. Most of the proposals involved:

- ◆ Guaranteed access to the Gulf for Iraq (a reasonable request, since the British set up Kuwait partly to block Iraq's access to the Gulf).
- ◆ Settling border disputes in the Rumaila oil field (95% in Iraq, 5% in Kuwait)
- ◆ A regional security arrangement.
- ◆ A plebiscite (vote) inside Kuwait.

Q: Are you saying that Saddam Hussein was a nice guy with reasonable demands and we simply misread his intentions?

A: I'm saying that if you tell Saddam Hussein (*or* Ariel Sharon) that he can have one piece of pie, he 'misunderstands' you and takes the whole pie. When you call him on it, *then* he gives you his list of reasonable requests. If your army is *stronger* than his, he settles for what he can get; if it's *weaker*, he thanks you for the pie.

The world would be a better place if guys like Saddam were suicidal but they seldom are. (If he had a death wish all he had to do was start something with Israel; I'm sure they'd be happy to oblige him.) Meanwhile, Secretary of State Baker and a coven of Diplomats couldn't get the American hostages back.

So Jesse Jackson & Muhammad Ali went over and pulled it off.

Nov 1, 1990— President Bush sends another 400,000 US soldiers to the Gulf but he doesn't want to tell the American people until after the Election because he's doing poorly enough in the Polls as it is

Nov 8,1990— Bush announces that he has just sent 400,000 more soldiers

Nov 10,1990— Poll: 75% of the people are against going to war even if sanctions fail

The Baker Girls

As the war was growing close, **Secretary of State Baker** came into his office only to find that some women were arguing with his men.

"Everyone says there's a fundamental difference in attitude between men and women on war and peace."

"You're right," replied **Janet Mullins**, his legislative chief: "Women do think differently. Women want to know that if their sons and daughters are going over there to die, it's not because their president ordered them there in a fit of pique." [*Newsweek, Jan 28, 1991*]

Nov 29, 1990—After much US pressure, UN authorizes the use of force
Dec 5, 1990— Israeli Foreign Minister **Levy** says Israel may attack Iraq!

The War Nobody Wanted..?

After the Geneva talks flopped the only hope we had of avoiding war was Congress. We knew our politicians too well to think they'd vote on principle against the most useless war in our country's history (Bush was right, it wasn't another Vietnam, it was much <u>dumber</u> than Vietnam), but they were mostly Democrats and this was a very Republican war.

Kuwait
Size: 6,880 sq.miles
Population: 1.8 million, 60% of whom are foreigners
Why Does Kuwait Exist:
Kuwait was part of Iraq's Basra Province until 1899 when Britain redrew its boundaries, divided it from Iraq and declared Kuwait its colony. Not long after that, it was "discovered" that Kuwait contained 10-20% of the world's oil reserves. In 1961, it was given its independence.
Who Rules? the Al-Sabah family, *period.*

Woody the AIPACker

Israeli spokesmen kept saying that this war had nothing to do with Israel, that Israel didn't want this war...but if that was the case, why did <u>Democratic</u> Rep. Stephen Solarz, an AIPAC [Israeli lobby] point man, work so hard convincing Congress—which was going to vote **against** the war—that Saddam Hussein thought we were bluffing and if he knew we were serious he'd back down in an instant. In what I consider the Slipperiest Logic in a decade, Solarz convinced Congress that the best way to **avoid** war was to vote **FOR** war.

(It frightens me to have my life in the hands of people that stupid.)

Congress voted for war so we got war.

Correction: *We* got Nintendo—*Iraq* got the war.

Not only didn't we *get* war, we weren't even allowed to *see* it.

Jan 16, 1991— America bombs Iraq.
Jan 17, 1991— America bombs Iraq.
Jan 18, 1991— America bombs Iraq.
Jan 19, 1991— America bombs Iraq.

Censorship

Our government told us that the war was censored for military reasons. They lied.

> The Pentagon did a study eight or ten years ago on Visual images. They found that the Visual Images that inflamed people most against a war were Civilian Casualties.
> The war was censored so we couldn't see what it was doing to the people of Iraq.

Newsweek, Jan.21: "The British...firmly believe that to enjoy public support, war must be conducted beyond the public's view."
("...to enjoy public support..!" If they ever build a Bullshit Museum, that quote will surely be in it.)

Finally, some little kids on the news had the heart to ask questions that the grown ups wouldn't touch: "But how do the other people feel? What do the other people say?"

The War in Iraq—the "Other" War, the "Other" People

If we bomb Iraq, we should at least have the guts and the respect to look at what it did to Iraq.

MYTH: "This has been fantastically accurate and that's because a lot of money went into this high technology weaponry— these laser guided bombs and a lot of other things— stealth technology—many of these technologies ridiculed in the past now coming into their own and saving lives, not only American lives, Coalition lives but the lives of Iraquis."

(It makes you want to rush right out and get bombed, doesn't it?)

That was how **President Bush** described our bombing raids.

REALITY: "It should be said at once that nothing we had seen or read had quite prepared us for the particular form of devastation which has now befallen the country. The recent conflict has wrought near-apocalyptic results upon the infrastructure* of what had been until January 1991, a highly urbanized and mechanized society. Now most means of modern life have been destroyed or rendered tenuous."

That was how the **UN Mission**, headed by **Under Secretary General Martti Ahtisaari**, described the results of our bombing raids after visiting Iraq in March 1991.

Infrastructure = the basic
things needed to keep your
city/country running—
electricity, water, sanitation,
roads, transportation, etc.

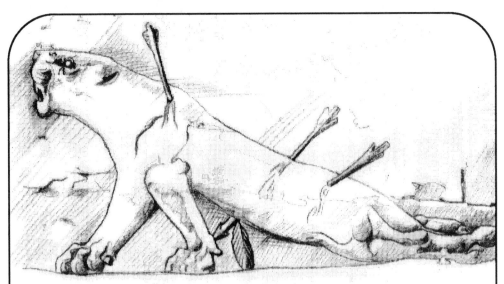

A Few Facts

- Best estimates are that 80 to 90% of the 'smart bombs' did hit their targest, but...
- Their targets were often exactly the things the civilian population needed to live: the smart bombs were aimed at—*and hit*—electricity, water, sanitation, roads, hospitals
- The 10 to 20% that went astray were devastating: One hit Fallujah, a city 40 miles from Baghdad. It killed 130 people. A 12-year-old boy, **Abdullah Mehsan**, now has stumps where his legs used to be. His father, uncle and cousin were killed in the raid.
- The *great* majority of the bombs were *dumb* bombs; the total of *all* bombs combined, *missed* their targets 70% of the time, often levelling entire blocks of civilian homes.

Voices: Anthropologist **Barbara Nimri Aziz** went to Iraq after the war. She played interviews with Iraquis on her **WBAI** [NY] radio show, *"TAHRIR: Voices of the Arab World"*. One interview was with an Iraqui sculptor named **Muhammad Abdul Ghani**.

Muhammad Abdul Ghani:

I was in America last year. I went to Washington for the International Conference of Sculpture and I went to New York. I was very happy. Very happy. I wished to come back again. But now I am very sad about what happened to us from the Americans. All Iraquis are very sad. If Bush and Saddam Hussein have trouble over politics, they should fix it in a *political way*—not bomb innocent people. Shame for America. Shame.

MYTH
◆ Iraq has 4th-largest [and/or 4th-strongest] army in the world.

FACTS
◆ Iraq's population is barely 50% larger than New York City's.
◆ America's Defense Budget [286 billion] is over seven times larger than Iraq's entire Gross National Product [40 billion].

Voices: Ms. Aziz's colleague **Laura Flanders** [who has her show: **"CrossCurrents,"** on WBAI, NY] interviewed the sculptor's daughter, **Hajar.** Hajar was a student at Baghdad University; she majored in English literature and spoke nearly perfect English.

Hajar Abdul Ghani:
I was crying...in the car...with my family...I see people around me, I see soldiers...they had to stand in trucks, they didn't have buses or cars to move them to...Kuwait...so, ohh...oh, when you look at them...faces...just young men... and you don't see smiles...young men, 17 or 18 or 20, well I started to laugh at them...and cry at the same time...

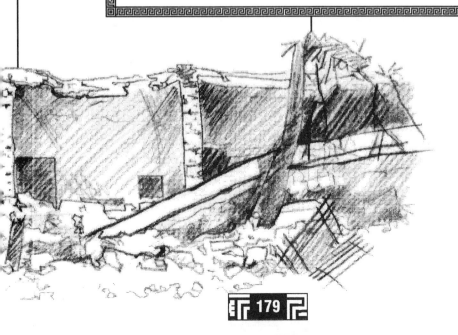

FACTS:
- ◆ We killed between 125,000 to 300,000 thousand Iraquis.
- ◆ We destroyed a 5,000 year-old city that was part of the whole world's history—part of our own history—and that I hear was once very beautiful.
- ◆ According to the *Harvard Report*, their conservative estimate is that by May of 1992 **170,000** Iraqui *children* under the age of five *will die* because of health problems directly related to the War. War? *What* war?
- ◆ You were more likely to be shot by another American soldier than by an Iraqui.
- ◆ Statistically, you stood a greater chance of getting killed *if you lived in New York* than if you were an American Soldier at "War" with Iraq.

FACT: Some of the "young men, 17, 18 or 20" that hurt Hajar Abdul Ghani to think about?

Described by Bill Moyers on PBS TV as "recent conscripts who had been forced to fight and never posed a threat to US forces during the war": about 25,000 were killed as they were trying to run away; another 8,000 of them were buried alive by US Army earth movers as they frantically tried to surrender. Colonel Anthony Moreno, part of the assault team, said, "What you saw was a bunch of buried trenches with people's arms and things sticking out of them."

> "Let me repeat, we have no argument
> with the people of Iraq.
> Indeed we have only friendship for the
> people there."
>
> **US President George Bush**, Nov.15, 1990

Voices:

Laura Flanders:
If you had one thing to say to the students of the United States, what would it be?

Hajar Abdul Ghani:
"I'd say, 'Please love us, because...we need love. We need someone to feel with us. We really don't hate Americans. We still like Americans. We...hate the way they treat us. We are not Saddam Hussein.

The Propaganda War:
Arab-Bashing in America

newsman Dan Rather, who defies every rule of fair
rnalism by attending Pro-Israeli functions.

A Propaganda CLASSIC

For weeks before America attacked Iraq one of my friends had been telling me about a movie he saw on TV. He said it was the main reason he and others we knew felt so strongly about destroying Saddam Hussein. One night he phoned to tell me the movie was on TV. If I watch the movie, he said, I will see that we have no choice but to bomb Iraq *now*. Our survival depends on it. After having seen the movie I'm amazed that, as far as I know, no media person acknowledges that it exists. It was on prime time TV *at least* two or three times in the weeks before the war. Many 'regular people' I know were moved by it, terrified by it, believed every word of it, and said it significantly affected how they felt about the War.

*On the surface, the movie was a documentary about **Nostradamus,** the 16th century French astrologer & physician famous for his prophecies. The first half of the movie presented Nostradamus as an infallible predictor of catastrophes, from Hitler to earthquakes. Absolutely infallible.*

The second half of the movie had some good news and some bad news.

The bad news was there's an Arab Muslim maniac in the Middle East who was preparing to nuke the entire Western world—that was the Prophecy.

The good news is, it isn't one of those etched-in-stone prophecies. If we go bomb the Arab Muslim maniac right now we can still save the world.

In other words, it was a Nazi propaganda movie aimed at Arabs, and narrated by Moses. Did I forget to mention that the narrator was Charlton Heston? I'm sure Charlton doesn't see any similarity between this and a Nazi propaganda film. Moses, baby, why would you do a thing like that?

'Anthing that makes Arabs look bad makes Israel look good.'

Dirty Money

"During the 1984 presidential campaign Walter Mondale responded to Jewish pressure by returning five thousand dollars he had received in contributions from four Arab Americans. A fifth contribution was returned to a woman because her name *sounded* Arabic. In 1986, James Abourezk, a former US Senator of Lebanese descent who is chairman of the Arab Anti-Discrimination Committee, sent a personal check for a hundred dollars to help Joseph Kennedy, the son of Robert F. Kennedy, in his Massachussetts campaign for Congress. One of Kennedy's aids, Steve Rothstein, returned the contribution, saying it was too "controversial".

The Arabs, by David Lamb

Your PATRIOTIC Duty

Arab-trashing was at its worst during the Gulf War. American Arabs who'd never seen the Middle East were attacked and insulted all across America. Mosques were bombed and burned and spray-painted with insults to Allah and Saddam "Insane".

The FBI questioned entire families because their heritage was Arabic.

But the hardest thing to take is what racism does to children. On **WBAI** [FM radio, NY] I heard Arab children who didn't understand why they were being humiliated by their classmates or told by their own teachers that they belonged to a bad and inferior race. Arab children were experiencing what African American children had gone through for hundreds years: they were suffering from and *becoming* the racist lies they were told about themselves.

(Probably because <u>those</u> dumb suckers believed the racist lies about THEMselves.)

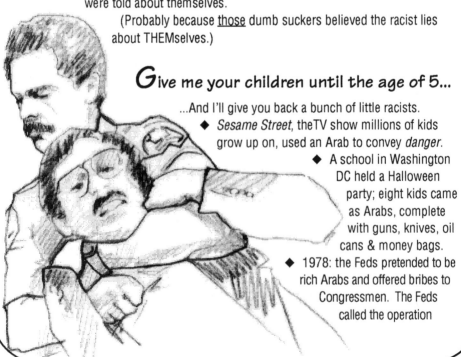

Give me your children until the age of 5...

...And I'll give you back a bunch of little racists.

◆ *Sesame Street*, theTV show millions of kids grow up on, used an Arab to convey *danger*.

◆ A school in Washington DC held a Halloween party; eight kids came as Arabs, complete with guns, knives, oil cans & money bags.

◆ 1978: the Feds pretended to be rich Arabs and offered bribes to Congressmen. The Feds called the operation

Abscam (Arab Scam). David Lamb [*The Arabs*] feels that if the Feds had called their operation Jewscam, or even blackscam, they'd have had a real situation on their hands.

"No matter," he writes. "The Arab is fair game, particularly on television."
Scholar Jack Shaheen thinks that TV has "discontinued pejorative characterizations" of other minorities, Arabs are still fair game. Shifty-eyes scumbags.

But Mr. Shaheen, you're missing the most unique aspect of anti-Arab racism.

Arabs in America

Racism against Arabs is *new*. Until 10 or 15 years ago Arabs were considered full-fledged human beings in America. You think that Arabs on TV haven't made their way up from cheap shots and racist stereotypes. The truth is, they've made their way *down* to cheap shots and racist stereotypes. A few years ago Arabs were *Mediterraneans* like Greeks and Italians. Now they're the only people you can make racial slurs about. Arabs, unlike any other people in America, have *become* a minority.

In the 50s and 60s Arabs were people. **Danny Thomas** had a corny sitcom with a guy called 'Uncle Tonoose' and Danny's daughter **Marlo** made a fine public transition from a cute little piece of fluff to an outspoken, dignified woman. Danny won an Emmy and put everyone to sleep with his St. Jude speech.

In the 1960's ["Lawrence of Arabia"] **Omar Sharif** came along and did a little image-adjusting for the Arabs. Omar was such a studly guy that in the 1968 movie "Funny Girl", **Barbara Streisand** played singer Fanny Brice, a pretty together lady except when she was near Nicky Arnstein, an irresistably sexy rascal who kept screwing up her life. I'm sure you remember who they chose to play Nicky Arnstein, the sexiest, studliest, most irresistible Jewish guy in town? Omar Sharif. An Egyptian. An *Arab*. Arabs were real people. There was no negative stigma attached to being an Arab OR a Moslem.

It's different now.

The 'DOZENS', Middle East Style

On the first day of the Madrid Peace Talks, Shamir (maybe his mind had been temporarily taken over by Martians) said "our quest for peace is unrelenting."

On day two Shamir reverted to his normal lovable self and blew a hole in the Peace Talks by accusing Syria of being a tyrannical regime.

Syria's well-prepared Foreign Minister responded by pulling out a 'Wanted' poster of Shamir, calling him a "Terrorist", and accusing him of murdering the UN Mediator Count Bernadotte.

At least they weren't lying.

Most people thought the Madrid Peace Talks were a failure. Not necessarily. Nobody badmouthed the other guy's mama. (*e.g*—the *classical* Dozens: 'Your mama is so ugly she ought to wear that turban around her face.') For peace talks they were a little rough; for a game of Dozens, they were downright polite.

from
The New York Times
Oct. 30, 1991

MIDEAST FOES VOICE GUARDED OPTIMISM ON PEACE PARLEY
A Palestinian Praises Israelis' 'New Tone'—Shamir Vows an 'Unrelenting' Quest
MADRID: On the eve of his nation's first peace conference with all its neighbors in four decades of hostility, prime Minister Yitzhak Shamir of Israel said..."

The Madrid 'DOZENS' & Shopping for Real Estate, Israeli Style

Syria

Size: 71,498 Sq.miles

Population: 12 million: 87% Muslim (mostly Sunni)

Who Rules: An elected President [currently Hafez Assad] with a partially elected/partially appointed People's Assembly [legislature].

How Created: In 1919 (with the blessing of Britain & France) Arab nationalists declared independence over all of Greater Syria but after World War I, the League of Nations (under the spiritual guidance of Britain & France) carved up Greater Syria into Palestine, Lebanon, Transjordan, and the present Republic of Syria.

Notes: Syrian nationalists were a major force in the Arab nationalist movement and the Arab Army that won independence from the Ottoman Empire—thereby helping the Allies win World War I. Their reward was several years of struggle against French armed occupation until France withdrew in 1946 after DeGaulle viciously bombed Damascus.

On November 13, 1971, General Hafez Assad took over. He's still there.

Speaking of Yitzhak Shamir...

Loan Guarantees—In September of 1992, Israeli Prime Minister Shamir asked the U.S. for a ten billion dollar "loan guarantee" (in addition to the billions we already give them).

"A group of Israeli **nationalists…!**" If a bunch of Arabs went into Brooklyn and threw six Jewish families out of **their** homes, do you think *The New York Times* would refer to them as Arab **nationalists**? That would probably be *The Times* first ever use of the F-word: "F_ _ _ing Arabs throw Jews out of six houses!"

On Our Land

While doing research at the Film Library, I discovered a documentary film made by some young Palestinians. In a style so restrained that it hurt to watch, the film **"On Our Land"** documented the fact that every day since they made themselves at home in Palestine, Zionists have been taking houses and land from whomever they want whenever they want.

In one very hard-to-watch scene, Israeli soldiers with bulldozers went into the Palestinian village of **Um al Fahm**. The man who owned the house stood there watching, smoking cigarette after cigarette, while the Israeli Army bulldozed his house until it was a pile of rubbish. "They can destroy my house," he said with tears running down his face, "but they will never destroy me."

Edward Said is a Palestinian/American writer, professor, political activist, avant garde book critic, classical music critic and general pain in the neck to Israel-fanatics because he's too smart for their good. Said was born in 1935, in Talbiya, a fancy Arab quarter of Jerusalem. He left with his family in 1947, shortly before Talbiya was overrun by Zionists.

In June of 1992, Said returned to Palestine. Except for a brief visit 25 years earlier, it was his first trip back. Using a map hand-drawn from memory by a friend, and carrying a copy of the title deed to his family's house, Said prowled the streets of Jerusalem. When, after two hours of searching, Edward Said found his family's old house, he lost track of himself. He was surprised when his daughter told him that, "using her camera with manic excitement, I reeled off twenty-six photos of the house."

Despite, or because of, all that passion, he couldn't go inside. Earlier, one of his friends had guided him through Jerusalem, explaining how Jewish settlers just took people's homes. In his article in *Harper's* (Dec.`92) Said wrote: "After lunch I visited a nearby home, where I was introduced to an elderly widow whose house had been summarily seized by a group of settlers. She now lived in the basement of the house, whose dark, airless interior was damp and unimaginably crowded although it did miraculously accomodate six or seven people."

"Another family I was introduced to told me of how they had come home one evening to find a lone settler wandering about inside their house. When asked what he thought he was doing he responded that he was there to look over `my house.'"

After reading things like those, I am struck above all by the incredible restraint of the Palestinian people.

Our congressmen are the finest
body of men that money can buy.

Morey Amsterdam

oney ◆ PACs ◆ Money ◆ PACs ◆ Money
◆ PACs Money ◆ PACs

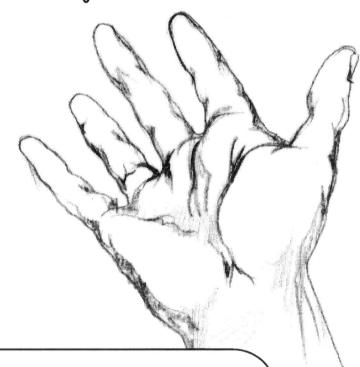

PACs (Political Action Committes) are those 'lobbies' you hear about. Everyone says they should be abolished. They rob part of our Democracy. Technically, PACs don't *bribe* our politicians, they just make extremely large "donations" to your "campaign".

If you play ball. If you *don't,* then they make extremely large donations to your opponent's "campaign". Both Bush and Clinton made pre-campaign promises to abolish them, but PACs are still here, more powerful than ever.

AIPAC's Power

◆ **AIPAC (American Israel Public Affairs Committee)** is the most powerful PAC in America. **AIPAC** is (to quote David Shipler, front page of *The New York Times*, July 6, 1987) "a major force in shaping United States policy in the Middle East," and that AIPAC has many members of the American government—what's the polite term for "in its pocket"?—and it isn't shy about using its power to make or break a politician's career. AIPAC even has "the power to influence a Presidential candidate's choice of staff".

(You can't imagine how that irritates me. I don't want the government of **ANY** other country to have **ANY** influence in our Democracy—least of all, a Loose Cannon like Israel. Stick around, it gets worse.)

◆ Shipler's article describes AIPAC's top men conferring with the-Secretary of State George Schultz, Schultz agreeing that the goal was "to build institutional arrangements so that eight years from now, if there is a Secretary of State who is not positive about Israel, he will not be able to overcome the bureaucratic relationships...that we have established." Terrifying.

◆ Jim Dine, AIPAC's mouthy director, embarrassed many American Jews (and pleased many others) by bragging that it was Jewish power, money and clout that beat **Senator Charles Percy**, the Illinois Republican who was such a prime time guy that he came very close to being the Republican nominee for President. (*Oh yeah it'll take a lot more than that to intimidate our lion-hearted politicians.*)

American Money

On the surface, America gives **three BILLION** dollars a year to Israel.

That's more than all of the other countries in the Middle East *combined*.

It's about $1,000 per Israeli civilian & $9,000 per Israeli soldier per year.

Both of which are more than most Americans get from our own government!

(This at a time when *more* Americans are *more* broke than at any time since the Depression! Why do we stand for it? Are we a bunch of sheep?)

"U.S. Aid to Israel: $77 Billion Since '67" [p10, *The NYTimes*, Sept 23,91]
77 BILLION! And that 77 Billion doesn't even include the *huge* amounts of "surplus" Military Equipment we *give* Israel, or the foreign aid subsidies or the assistance to refugees arriving from Russia. Or the "Loans."

The Great Loan Guarantee' Debate

President Bush's response to Shamir's loan guarantee request was, We'll give you the Loan Guarantee if you stop building new Jewish settlements in the Occupied Territories. PM Shamir said essentially, Wise up, bonehead—that's why we want the money!—and mentioned for the millionth time "Israel's perfect loan repayment record". Bush held his ground but everybody knew that one way or the other, Israel would get the money. Especially with "Israel's perfect loan repayment record".

Shamir wasn't joking—Israel *does* have a Perfect Loan-Repayment Record.
I only recently found out why.

The Disgusting Truth about Israel's Loan Repayment Record

There are two reasons for Israel's perfect loan-repayment record:

◆ Between 1974 and 1989, military loans totalling $16.4 billion were turned into "grants"—gifts! We 'forgave' the loan. (That was a sneaky way to increase Israel's "aid" to 4.5 billion a year without people noticing.)

◆ The second reason for Israel's perfect loan-repayment record (this is unreal) is, since 1984, **because of an amendment by Senator Alan Cranston (D-CA),** America's economic aid to Israel "shall not be less than the annual debt repayment (interest and principal) from Israel to the United States government."

This information is from a Congressional Research Service study reported by Sheldon L. Richman in his article, "The Economic Impact of the Israeli Loan Guarantees", *Journal of Palestine Studies*, Winter, 1992.

In other words, Israel's loan repayment record is PERFECT because
the American tax payers, pay it!

NOTE: In 1985 AIPAC 'donated' **$182,982 to Senator Alan Cranston's** 'campaign.'
Do you know what REALLY hurts? WE PAID Senator Alan Cranston to screw us.

Why isn't there open debate over Foreign Aid to Israel?
I'd be willing to bet that the American people are tired of giving money to Israel.

NOTE: According to our own laws, we canNOT give Foreign Aid to any country that builds nuclear weapons illegally—which Israel does. (See the **Vanunu Case** in the next chapter.)

One last teaspoon of salt in the wound: America sent Patriot missles <u>and</u> American soldiers to Israel during the Gulf War; <u>and Israel sent us a bill for 13 BILLION dollars!</u>

Do you know what we've bought with that money?
7,000 dead Jews, 100,000-200,000 dead Arabs and **750 million new enemies.** Muslims everywhere now feel that America places no value on Muslim life.

190

The World Trade Center Bombing & The Mother of ALL Propaganda Wars

Christian "Islamic Fundamentalists"

In December 1992, Israel's new Prime Minister Yitzhak Rabin threw 415 Palestinians out of Gaza. He said the expulsions were "a necessary blow against Islamic fundamentalists."
NOTE: about 15 of the Islamic Fundamentalists were <u>Christians!</u>

A couple days before the end of February, 1993, an explosion rocked the World Trade Center in New York. Within minutes , New York TV stations were filled with guessing games and speculations. A guy from Channel 4 who was so white it hurt to look at him had gone off the deep end and was assuring us it was a terrorist bomb despite the fact the official people said it was "just" an explosion.

He was right. I was surprised when the first names I heard mentioned were Croats and the Serbs, but within seconds [as I expected] the word `Arab' (like it had a little magnet up its nose) attached itself to the word `Terrorist.'

While the experts traded opinions, I tried to reason my way into it.

I usually start with the question, "Who benefits from it?"

The reason I felt pretty sure it *wasn't* an Arab—especially not a Palestinian—was because in the last few weeks there was great public sympathy for the deported Palestinians—and a lot of world anger at the Israelis. (Which they somehow always manage to dodge.) Then, within hours, I heard an announcement that, because of their greater experience with terrorist bombs [like the King David Hotel?] an Israeli bomb crew was going to help our guys solve the case.

The Arabs would be blamed even if they didn't do it. I was sure of it.

"If You Don't Behave..."

In the days after the bombing the media people went into a speculation frenzy. Every car-bomber or terrorist, group or freelance, real or imagined during the last 100 years was suspect—in particular some disgusting new beast—maybe it had four heads and ate babies. They called it the "**Islamic Fundamentalists.**" (You could imagine mothers all over the world telling their disobedient children, 'If you don't behave, I'll get the *Islamic Fundamentalists* after you.')

Within days the FBI/NY Police cracked the case. In no time at all seven suspects —*Islamic Fundamentalists* from *Brooklyn* and *New Jersey*—were in custody.

And a blind *Islamic Fundamentalist* preacher was probably the ring leader!

The MOSSAD is Israel's CIA. They'd be insulted by that definition because they think they're better than the CIA.

One of their famous cases— featured on "60 Minutes" and made into a movie—was the Vanunu Case. Mordechai Vanunu worked in an Israeli plant that made nuclear bombs—very illegal. His conscience bothered him so he went to England and spilled the beans.

In October 1986 the London Sunday Times published Vanunu's revelation that Israel had already made 100-200 nuclear bombs. Vanunu, with the help of the British, went into hiding. The Mossad found him, sent a beautiful woman to entice him to a place where they could kidnap him. Vanunu is now in an Israeli prison and the Mossad has been elevated to an almost mythical level.

Jewish Ninjas

However, some people smelled something fishy...

Alexander Cockburn, writing in *The Nation* and **Nabeel Abraham** in *Lies of our Times* both wondered why neither the police nor the media had mentioned **Mossad**? (They were one of the best car bombers around—and all that bad press that Israel had been getting—*what* deported Palestinians?—suddenly disappeared.) Not only had they not mentioned Mossad, but...let's go one step at a time.

Mohammed Salameh was one of the first people arrested. According to the Official Complaint read at his court hearing, when Salameh rented the famous van, he gave as a reference the name and phone number of **Guzie Hadass**. The police/FBI got the address that belonged to that phone number and, sure enough, when they got there they found a letter addressed to Salameh, plus "tools and wiring, and manuals concerning antennae, circuitry and electromagnetic devises. (**Jane Hunter**, using the official court complaint as her reference [from *Middle East International,* Mar.19,'91]).

Ms. Hunter was a little shocked when she read what FBI spokesman Joe Valiquette told the *Herald Tribune* [Mar 8]: *"We have no idea whether Hadass is a member of the Israeli Mossad, but even if it were true, we wouldn't tell you anyway."*

The plot thickens: Salameh's circle of Muslims overlapped with **Sayyid Nosair's**, the guy who had been charged with killing **Rabbi Meir Kahane**, leader of the violent Jewish Defense League.

A friend asked me a question that might occur to you so let's deal with it now. Some time after Rabbi Kahane went to Israel and became a member of Israel's Knesset [Congress], my friend said, "What is an American doing in <u>Israel's</u> government?"

The answer would be obvious if it weren't for Israel's advertising campaign.

'Ancient' Israel isn't even as old as California, so everyone born after 1948 is from another country. There's no such thing as a native-born Israeli over the age of 45.

Rabbi Kahane's son claims [*Inside Israel,* Feb.] that "both the FBI and Mossad had infiltrated the group to which Nosair belonged." **Benjamin Kahane** says he was told by an FBI informant he identifies as Mustafa Shalabi that Nosair's brother worked for the FBI" [Hunter, *Middle East International.*]

Shalabi (who later turned up dead) had worked with **Sheik Omar Abdel Rahman**—the blind preacher.

IN OTHER WORDS—It looked like the media and the FBI/Police had been trying awfully hard to link Salameh and Nosair—*and* to avoid looking into links to the FBI or Mossad. Even if Mossad or the FBI or the CIA hadn't done the bombing, they may have been (or hired) '*agents provocateurs*'. (In the 60s you heard a lot about '*agents provocateurs*', guys hired to *provoke* young 'radicals', who talked a good game but never did anything, into doing something so you could arrest them. P*rovocateurs* were illegal.)

Q: What exactly are you saying here?
I'm saying, look into *all* reasonable possibilities.
Then punish the bad guys, *whoever they are*.

But so far, it looks like we have already found guilty:

Seven-guilty-until-proven-innocent-Arab-Islamic-Suspects
One blind man.
And, above all, Islam.

I can't say who is or isn't guilty—I don't know any more than you do.
But I do know that Americans of all people, should know better than to be trashing someone else's religion, carrying on a Propaganda War against Islam.

Not only were Arabs blamed for the World Trade Center Bombing, but ISLAM was insulted in ways that only the most hardcore antiSemites insulted Judaism.

Israeli politician Benjamin Netanyahu, in his book *Terrorism: How the West Can Win*, states that Arabs have "a disposition toward unbridled violence. This can be traced to a world view which asserts that certain ideological and religious goals justify, indeed demand, the shedding of all moral inhibitions."

He draweth out the thread of his verbosity finer than the staple of his argument.
Shakespeare, *Love's Labor's Lost*

I agree, Uncle Willie, but it's the staple of his argument that bothers me. If you said that Jews had "a disposition toward unbridled violence" you'd be put on the list with Eichmann!

Yes But, Islam Has an Image Problem

For one thing it seems so serious.
Where is the sense of humor in Islam?"

Nobody's holy book is
humorous.
The humor is in the
people. Or in the
secular literature.
Muslims are exactly like everyone
else.
But a little irreverence wouldn't
hurt Islam's image.

The most ridiculous thing about the
Propaganda War against Islam during the World Trade
Center Bombing was that we were in the midst of one of the most
outrageously fundamentalist Christian groups in Whacko, Texas. . .while for
years we've seen Zionist Jews with Bibles in one hand & Uzis in the other.

Not to mention the fact that the very premise of Israel's existence is:
God gave it to me!

That's as fundamentalist as it gets.
I hope he doesn't give you anything of mine.
Joseph Campbell (the generous spirited mythographer who understood the common
goal of all of our religions & saw the beauty of all of our myths) believed that ALL our
religions, and ALL of our myths serve the same purpose.

I like that.

I don't read anything like a True Believer—that includes the Old & New Testaments
and the Koran. I don't suspend my judgment for anybody, including Gods and
Prophets. I'm going to tell it as I see it...
! don't presume to know whose god is God—or who He talks to.
My religion is Democracy—
Whoever God is, He gets one vote just like the rest of us.

And besides...

"It isn't what God says, it's what you hear."

I may be wrong but I feel at the core of Islam a great sense of honor.
I think it has a great potential for heroism.

A religion is its people. Here are two of them you've already met.
A king and a sculptor.

There is a story about Jordan's King Hussein that Annie Dillard tells in her book, *The Writing Life*. (Read her version; these few lines don't do it justice.)

At different times and places, Ms. Dillard and King Hussein became fascinated with a stunt pilot named Dave Rahm. Dillard and Hussein couldn't be more different—she's a no-nonsense American writer, he's the King of Jordan and a direct descendant of Muhammad!—yet they both found the flying of Dave Rahm so unutterably beautiful... "It was as if Mozart could move his body through his notes, and you could walk out on the porch, look up, and see him in periwig and breeches, flying around in the sky."

Dave Rahm was flying at an air show in Jordan. Dave's wife Katy was sitting with Hussein in the viewing stands when Dave's airplane didn't come out of a spin and nosedived into the ground and exploded. King Hussein rushed to the burning plane to pull his friend out but Dave Rahm was dead.

Barbara Aziz interviewed Muhammad Abdul Ghani some months later at his studio:

Aziz: Muhammad Abdul Ghani is the pre-eminent sculptor in Baghdad. He studied for years in Italy, I see Shaharazade, the 40 thieves, and other pieces of his work.

(To him) They can hear your voice, they can hear your *spirit* as an artist and as an Iraqui person. This is not a person who is just going to lie down and go away. We're here in your studio. You have a new project underway. I see models.

Muhammad Abdul Ghani: Yes it came at a perfect time for me. We have many churches in Iraq, especially in Baghdad.

Aziz: You have a Christian population here in the city?

Ghani: Of course. We have them as friends. They live here for thousands of years and we live together in a *good* way. So they are building a Catholic new church and the architect chose me. It's very interesting that they chose me as a Muslim man to do this subject for the Christian Church. We have no problem really. I imagine to do murals about the story of Jesus Christ. I put lots of people around the religious subjects. I was very sad about what happened to Jesus Christ—very sad—as a human being, but I made all these people around him...were very sad, too...very sad. Maybe on the inside of myself I am presenting the people around me, very very sad.

Aziz: The Lower Panel is a scene of Jesus taking up the cross. On the Upper Panel, many people, men, women and children, are looking down.

Ghani: I imagine that Jesus Christ carried the cross. At the same time, I imagine that the people on the street looking to him, looking to him. Standing, lookin, crying, sad.

Sad for <u>him</u>. This sadness are the people here, now, around me. What I am seeing here, now...all around me.

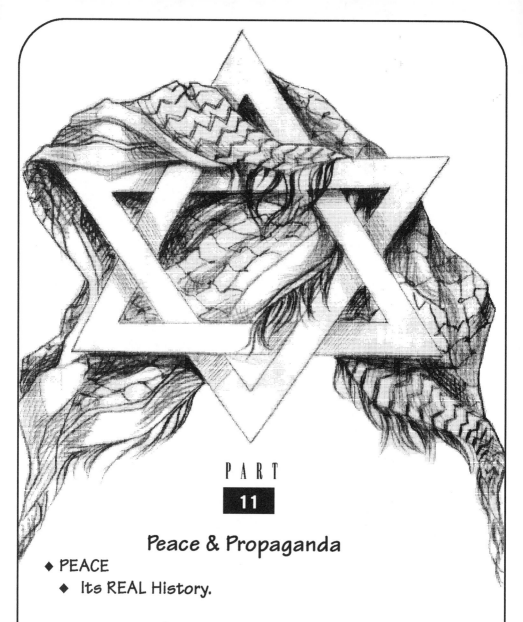

PART
11

Peace & Propaganda

- ◆ PEACE
  - ◆ Its REAL History.

  - ◆ Israel & PLO sign a Peace Treaty!
    What EXACTLY did they agree to?
    Why are so many Palestinians & Israelis so angry?
    Is AUTONOMY the same as a PALESTINIAN STATE?
    Prospects, Pitfalls, Problems...
        ARAFAT ARAFAT ARAFAT...what have you done
- ◆ MY Opinion:
    Lo Chaim—"To Life", To PEACE...

> "Who controls the past controls the future;
> Who controls the present controls the past."
>
> *George Orwell, 1984*

EACE

The REAL History of PEACE Between Arabs & Israel

◆ **MYTH:** All Israel wants is to live in Peace. But the Arabs want to push us into the sea.

◆ **REALITY:** In 1977 the PLO offered Israel a full peace treaty. Israel said No.

◆ Later in 1977 the US and Russia got together and issued a joint peace proposal. The PLO accepted it [Oct '77] but the Israelis griped until the US dropped it.

◆ Nov. 1978: Arafat told Rep. Paul Findley he wanted to talk peace with the US. Arafat's statement: "The PLO will accept an independent Palestinian state consisting of the West Bank and Gaza, with connecting corridor, and in that circumstance will renounce any and all violent means to enlarge the territory of that state. I would reserve the right, of course, to use nonviolent means, that is to say, diplomatic and democratic means, to bring about the eventual unification of all Palestine." "We will give de facto recognition to the State of Israel." The Israelis ignored him. Arafat offered Israel *everything* they said they wanted...and they wouldn't even talk to him?

◆ In 1982 Saudi Arabia, Iraq, Syria and Jordan all offered peace. Israel ignored them.

◆ Israeli writer Amos Elon said that "Sadat's *famous* 1971 peace offer" (that Americans never heard about), caused "panic and unease among our political leadership."

There are many more instances—I counted 17 in 15 pages of Chomsky's 480 page *The Fateful Triangle*—but I trust I've made my point.

◆ If you're getting the impression that Arafat was Mother Teresa, forget it: Arafat definitely <u>was</u> a terrorist, especially in the early days, but from the mid-70s on, he made peace offer after peace offer that were not only rejected by the Israelis, but **The New York** *All-the-news-that's-fit-to-print* **Times** didn't bother mentioning them. So Americans didn't even know about them—*unless they read <u>Israeli</u> newspapers!*

Not only were Americans "protected from" 17 years worth of Arab peace offers but you can do an awful lot of looking and—unless you're lucky enough to look in the right place—you'll never find them. The Arab peace offers, like many other indisputable, true facts that make the Arabs look good or Israel look bad, have disappeared from History.

[People who find this stuff hard to believe—as *I* once did—should take a look at Chapter 3, pages 39-80, of Noam Chomsky's painstakingly documented, scrupulously fair book, *The Fateful Triangle*.]

◆ **REALITY and REJECTIONISM:** To the best of my knowledge, in the 40-some years of its existence, Israel has never made a peace offer to the Arabs. US President Carter nearly had to put a gun to Begin's head to get him to sign a treaty with Egypt's Sadat.

The peace offer Sadat originally 'brought to the table' was "comprehensive": it offered a Full Peace Treaty between **Israel** and **Egypt** *and* **Syria** *and* **Jordan** *and* the **PLO**! Israel refused, insisting that any further talks be limited to Egypt. The US conceded.

Kissinger made a secret agreement with Israel that the US would not <u>*talk*</u> to the PLO.

Who Speaks for You

◆ Stupid question, right? You speak for yourself. Stupid as it sounds, that's been one of the key problems for years. As usual, the problem was one-sided: the Palestinians would talk to anybody. The Israelis, hard headed and self righteous for a change, refused to talk to the PLO. By the mid-70s, the constant threat of peace had made Israelis a little irritable. 1976 when Syria called for a special session of the UN Security Council, the Israelis refused to attend. The Labor Party Government, headed by **Yitzhak Rabin** announced that it would *not* negotiate with *any* Palestinian on *any* political issue, and it would NOT negotiate with the PLO *even if the PLO renounced terrorism and recognized Israel!*

'Are you lost daddy?' I asked tenderly.
'Shut up,' he explained.

Ring Lardner

STOP EVERYTHING!
The PLO/Israeli PEACE Agreement

Part of me asks, '*Why? After all these years, why NOW?*'
Part of me says, 'Who gives a damn Why? Just so they <u>do</u> it. Yitzhak Rabin *looks like he means it* when he says he wants Peace!

Let's have a hand for Rabin.
And Arafat? Let's give him a hand before someone kills him.
The things I've heard about Arafat...they break your heart. For *him,* <u>and</u> for his people.

HEROS: In Decmeber 1992, Israeli History professor **Yair Hirschfeld** and **Ahmed Kriah,** head of the PLO's *economics* department arranged, with great secrecy from their own governments, to meet in a London hotel to see if there was any way for two men without much influence to jump-start the peace process. They were sure nothing would come of it but they kept trying. The meetings, 14 of them during the next eight months, moved to **Oslo, Norway.** Most of the meetings were held at the home of Norway's Foreign Minister **Johan Jorgen Holst** and his wife **Marianne.** Holst and Marianne (she led a study group in the Occupied Territories) not only provided hospitality and moral support, they both became key figures in the talks.

Meetings that would have been tense anywhere else—Israelis & Palestinians trying to ignore history and trust each other, exhausted from working all night hammering out agreements that both sides can live with—became evenings with friends, a little food, a little wine and a little boy. The guests felt so much at home that they thought nothing of crawling around on the floor with the Holst's four-year-old son **Edvard**! (Edvard even played with *Arafat* when the Holsts went to Tunisia!) To a man, they felt sure that the talks would never have succeeded if they'd been held anyplace else.

ANNOUNCEMENTS: On August 20, Israeli Foreign Minister **Shimon Peres** went to Oslo to witness the initialing of the Declaration of Principles. On August 27, Peres and Holst flew to California to brief US Secretary of State **Warren Christopher**. Christopher called President Clinton. No one could believe it.

On August 29, 1993, to the great surprise of nearly everyone in the world, Israel and the PLO announced that they'd come to an agreement on Palestinian self-rule.

Damn near everyone in the world was amazed. I know I was.

Even more amazing, they were going to sign documents "acknowledging each others' existence." (You wonder how two guys who've been dodging each other's bullets for 25 years could doubt each other's existence... but that's the wrong tone for this event. It's a major breakthrough.)

Professor **Yair Hirschfeld** and **Ahmed Kriah** deserve the Nobel Peace Prize. If they have a couple of spares, **Johan Jorgen Holst** and his wife **Marianne** could use them.

The PHOTO-OP Doctrine: Shortly after **President Clinton** took the do-rag off his hair, he phoned Prime Minister **Yitzhak Rabin** and invited Mr. Rabin to have the formal signing of his Declaration of Principles at the White House. You can tease the Prez all you want but that turned out to be a great idea. Yitzhak Rabin was an old soldier—he *hated* making peace with the PLO. He did it because it was good for Israel. But he didn't have to like it. He disliked it so much that he *wasn't even going to attend the signing* of his own crowning achievement. When the President called and personally asked Prime Minister Rabin to come to the signing, Rabin said Yes, just like that.

Yitzhak Rabin's presence was important: it made the document more important, it made Arafat more important and it made peace more important.

The Agreement—What EXACTLY Does it AGREE To? And WHEN?

No one knows for sure. That's one reason why it makes people—especially Palestinian people—so nervous. I'll outline the program first and talk about the questions afterward.

The Declaration of Principles

In the most basic sense, **The Declaration of Principles** is a plan to give Palestinians <u>control</u>, little by little, over <u>land</u>** in the Occupied Territories.
In both cases—<u>Land</u> & <u>Control</u>—you *start small* and *work your way up*, bit by bit.

Oct. 13, 1993

◆ Palestinians begin taking [fairly complete] control of the **Gaza Strip** & **Jericho**

◆ Palestinians begin "Early Empowerment" [very limited control] in the rest of the West Bank: control of Education & Culture, Health & Social Welfare, and Direct Taxation (NOTE: if you don't know exactly what all that stuff means, don't feel bad—nobody else does either.)

◆ Tourism is transferred from Israel to "authorized Palestinians" in West Bank & Gaza

◆ Palestinians build Police Force using PLO fighters from outside the West Bank & Gaza

◆ An Israeli-Palestinian Economic Cooperation Committee is formed to work on water, electricity, energy, finance, transport, etc

◆ Jordan & Egypt are invited to join a Continuing Committee to decide how to handle Palestinians [800,000] displaced from West Bank & Gaza

   ◆ In 4 to 6 months, Palestinians take over the **Administration** of **Gaza** & **Jericho**

   ◆ The Israeli Army *leaves Gaza & Jericho;* a *Palestinian Police Force* replaces them

   ◆ The Israeli Army is responsible for External Security & Protection of Jewish settlements inside Gaza & Jericho

Dec. 13, 1993

◆ Five-year interim period of Palestinian self-rule officially begins.

July 13, 1994

◆ Latest date for Palestinian Council; Palestinians from East Jerusalem will be able to vote [and perhaps run] in the Elections

◆ Israeli Army [already gone from Gaza & Jericho] would move away from areas highly populated by Palestinians; they would be gone by the day before the elections; Israeli forces would be responsible for Israeli settlers

Dec. 13, 1995

◆ Latest date for talks to start on permanent agreement

Dec. 13, 1998

◆ Permanent agreement takes effect. Polls taken in Israel and the Occupied Territories show that about 55% of both Palestinians & Israelis are in favor of the plan. However: 70% of the Palestinians in the Gaza Strip & Jericho—the first two areas to change hands—favored the Peace Plan. No big surprise.

What Do PALESTIANS Object To?

They have three *general* objections: it leaves them subordinate to Israel; it doesn't mention some important matters & it's too vague on others. Some specific objections:

1. Independent Palestinian State or "**Autonomy**"—The Palestinians want an independent Palestinian State. A real **Democracy**. What the Israelis offer is **Autonomy**. Nobody is certain what the Israelis mean by Autonomy. One version of Autonomy is Indians living on a reservation, so Palestinians should be edgy—they want to know where the Document that's going to determine their future is heading? One thing is sure: if the Israelis *meant* 'an independent Palestinian State', they would have *said* 'an independent Palestinian State'.

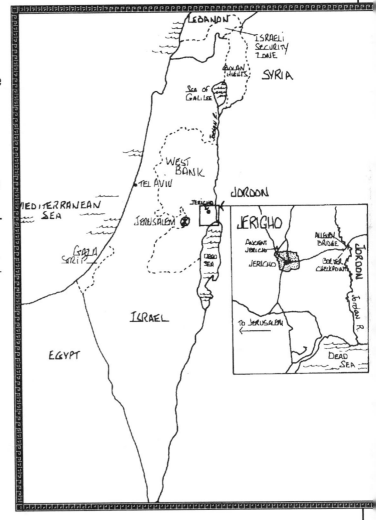

2. How MUCH Land?—This agreement is among other things, "A Land for Peace" offer—'I give you land if you stop fighting.' You don't need a Degree from Harvard to know that your next question is, 'How much land?' They've put their lives on the line...and they want to know exactly what they're trading it for.

3. Waiting **5 years for Self-Rule**—they think it's too long.

4. What happens to **Jerusalem**?

5. What happens to the **Jewish settlers** [137,000] in the Occupied Territories?

6. What happens to the nearly 2 million **Palestinians** who do *not* live in the Occupied Territories? Do they have any rights of Compensation or Return?

7. What happens to the 13,000 **political prisoners** in Israeli jail, many of whom are held, indefinitely, secretly and with having been charged with any crime?

What Do ISRAELIS Object To?

1. Security—That's by far the main prioity with most Israelis. For Israelis living in the Occupied Territories, more than a concern. And the possibility, no matter how unlikely, that the PLO might rebuild & resume its old ways.

2. That **"Autonomy"** <u>will</u> turn into **An independent Palestinian State!**

Where Are the PROBLEMS Likely to Come From?

Israelis & Palestinians both seem determined to take responsibility for keeping order among their own people, so some of the worst clashes may not be between Israelis & Palestinians, but Israeli against Israeli, and Palestinian against Palestinian.

What's going to happen if the Israeli Army 'asks' a settlement of Gush Emunim Jews—the guys with a Bible in one hand and a machine gun in the other who think they're doing God's work—to move out of the Territories?

What's going to happen when the new PLO Police Force in Gaza has to go into the poverty-stricken refugee camps to arrest or confront members of Hamas on their own turf?

And what's going to happen to Arafat? Palestinian anger and disappointment doesn't seem to be directed at the Israelis, it seems to be aimed at Yasir Arafat. (The PLO, too, but mainly Arafat.) Not just the anger of the fanatics, but the anger of sane, gentle people. And the sense of betrayal.

Full Circle

I'll end this book the same way I started: with my Opinions, not Facts. First, a few comments on the new Peace Offer from people I respect:

Alexander Cockburn: "...Rabin and Peres...plucked Arafat and his PLO from the grave and guided his hand through the articles of surrender..." "Study the exchanges between Rabin and Arafat, and it is plain that Israel commits to nothing..." "Right now, Palestinians get the right to manage the world's largest prison, the Gaza Strip, plus one cow town."

Christopher Hitchens: "Earlier in the week...I had sat down with Ilan Halevi, one of the two Jewish members of the PLO visiting team.... He told me that the joke in the delegation, when confronted with the Gaza offer, was to say: 'O.K., we accept. But what will you give us in exchange?'"

PEACE—YES or NO? Have they made any *real* progress toward peace? (Or is this what Moshe Dayan meant when an American diplomat asked him in 1988 if Israel thought anyone was dumb enough to accept a "Gaza First" offer instead of an overall solution, Dayan answered, "We'll double-cross that bridge when we come to it.")

I believe that it *is* real progress toward peace. But it's not like tearing down the Berlin Wall—it's like removing ten or twelve bricks. If it is progress, it's the kind that inches its way toward a solution that is still five or fifty years—and thousands of lives—and billions and *billions* and BILLIONS of dollars away.

DO YOURSELF A FAVOR and buy a copy of the October '93 *Lies of Our Times,* and read **Jeffrey Blankfort**'s article, "Blank Check to Israel". These are a few highlights:

"On June 17, 1993, by a 309-to-111 vote, the House of Representatives passed a $13-billion foreign aid bill (H.R.2295) that will maintain economic and military assistance for Israel at its $3-billion level and provide nearly $1 billion in additional off-budget bonuses."

The Israelis take it for granted that they'll get that money (or *more*) forever. *The New York Times* knows that Americans aren't happy about giving all that money to Israel when the US is so broke. Their solution? "February 1989...was the last time the *New York Times* ran a story describing Congress's role in approving aid to Israel.

"Last year, the *Times* Washington correspondent, Adam Clymer, wrote a ten-inch article on the foreign aid vote without indicating that Israel was again the top money-winner... This year, Clymer ignored the story completely."

Other major newspapers also chose not to mention US aid to Israel. **Personally,** I would rather flush that money down the toilet than give it to Israel. As long as Israel assumes that it has to have a stronger army than all the Arab countries combined, there will be a war whenever Israel wants to shrink one of the Arab armies. When it's possible, Israel will con some other country into destroying its enemy (America is still trying to figure out why we went to war with Iraq).

Check out Yitzhak Rabin's February 18, 1990 address to the Knesset (Israeli Congress) as reported the next day by Dan Margalit in *Ha'aretz*. In reference to the Gulf War, he said, "because of a miracle, a foreign army is fighting our worst enemy for our sakes".

If the future is like the past, Israel will blame each of those wars on the Arabs, supporters of Israel will pump more anti-Arab propaganda *into* America and take more money *from* America.

At least when you flush money down the toilet it doesn't hurt anybody.

Do you know what we've bought with all the billions of dollars we've given to Israel? The table below is lower than a "conservative estimate"

A SUMMARY OF THE FIRST 45 YEARS OF THE ARAB-ISRAELI CONFLICT

	Jews	Total Arabs	Palestinans	Lebanese	Syrians	Egyptians	Jordanians	Others
1939 Riots	329	3,293	3,293					
1948-49 War	2,000	thousands	thousands					
1950s	0	96	28	25		43		
1967 War	778	20,000+			3,500	12,000	entire army	34 Americans
1973 War	2,552	15,000			total=	15,000		110 Lib.Airline
1978 Inv.Leb.	0	2,000		2,000				
1982 Inv.Leb	487	30,000+	15,000+	15,000+				
1982-92				thousands				
Intifada to '89	85	900	900					
fr/Terrorists				400				
SUBTOTAL	6,212	67,323++						

What Do I Want?

Although I dont' think that Israel benefits anyone, *including the Jewish people*, I don't expect Israel to quit the Middle East. <u>So what do I want?</u>

I want a few famous American Jews, especially ones I respect like Philip Roth, Susan Sontag, Norman Mailer, Grace Paley [you already do most of it], Woody Allen, Max Apple, Doctorow, and dozens of others—all of, the people who've taught me everything I knew, to stand up and say, "Let's quit lying to the world—and to ourselves.

We stole Palestine. We stole it. Even if we give the Palestinians 'autonomy', or 'self-determination' or the 'West Bank', or a Palestinian State, we will still have stolen most of their country.

Let's at least start off by telling the truth.

RECOMMENDED READING: Life doesn't end where this book ends. The intent of this book is not only to tell you the truth about the past, it's to help you to find the truth in the future. I've given you some background, now I'll point you in the direction of people & places who'll give you the "most factual" facts about Arabs and Israelis. The rest is up to you.

The BEST 'Single-Author' BOOKS

◆ *The Fateful Triangle* by **Noam Chomsky** is, by a mile, the best general (*somewhat* scholarly) book on the Arab/Israeli conflict from the beginning of Zionism (*c.* 1900) to Israel's 1982 invasion of Lebanon. It is a great reference/browsing book but most people (including me) find it hard to read straight through. It's 480 pages, full of notes, many of which are as good as the text. Chomsky is the fairest writer I've ever read. No matter what he writes about, he judges both sides by the same standards.

◆ *Taking Sides* by **Stephen Green.** To get the facts right for his 1988 book, Stephen Green went to the National Archives to examine our State Dept's declassified 1948-67 "Israel file". The first thing that amazed Mr. Green was that he was *the first and only person* who had ever asked to look at the official files! The second thing that amazed him were the facts: "In poring through the files, seeing the communications about the ambushes and bombings. . .I could see that what I was reading was not the heroic stuff of a very fictional *Exodus*, nor even that of some of the more recent 'nonfiction' on the birth of Israel. *The reality was so different from the myth as to be unrecognizable.*" Unfortunately, the book only covers the period from 1948 to 1967.

◆ *Israel's Lebanon War* by **Ze'ev Schiff & Ehud Ya'ari.** This is the definitive account of Israel's 1982 invasion of Lebanon. As you read it, keep two things in mind: 1. the Israeli Army censored 20-50% of the original manuscript; 2. on a gut-level, the authors are so pro-Israeli that they refer to *all* Palestinians as "the terrorists."

◆ *While Six Million Died* by **Arthur D. Morse.** It should be required reading in every school in America. Nearly every country in the world stood by without lifting a hand while the Nazis killed six million Jews. Sometimes I think that no non-Jew can ever know what it feels like to be Jewish. (I don't know what follows from that.)

◆ *The Question of Palestine* by **Edward W. Said** is passionate and scholarly but ultimately very sad. (These 'reviews' are *opinions*, not facts.) It's as if Edward Said, a smart and sensitive (to say the least) man has been put in a position where he has to waste half of his life documenting the fact that he *exists*. Why? Because he's *Palestinian*. Part of the mythology of modern Israel is to deny the existence of Palestine and Palestinians. Israel—and the intellectual thugs in America who support it—are trying to rub Palestine out of history. The soldier resists genocide in one way, the scholar in another. (Yes, *genocide*.) What Arafat & the Intifada say with their actions, Said says with footnotes: *we exist.*

◆ *A Concise History of the Middle East,* by **Arthur Goldschmidt, Jr.** takes on the enormous task of covering the Middle East from the time before Muhammad to the present. It deserves its reputation as the most widely used general textbook on the subject.

◆ *The Cartoon History of the Universe* by **Larry Gonick** is brilliant & fun.

The Best 'COLLECTIONS'

◆ *For Palestine* edited by **Jay Murphy** contains essays by some of the best thinkers & most important players in the Middle East, including Noam Chomsky, Edward Said and Hanan Ashwari, the Palestinian peace negotiaor.

◆ *Blaming the Victims* edited by **Edward Said & Christopher Hitchens** contains the most deeply felt essays I've ever read by Chomsky and Said. It also features a platoon of young Palestinian scholars who, piece by piece, prove that Palestine exists (or exist<u>ed</u>). One of the brightest of the young scholars, Rashid Khalidi, appears on TV occasionally and writes articles in *The Journal of Palestine Studies*.

The Biggest SURPRISE

◆ Check out the entry under "Palestine" in the *Encyclopedia Britannica*. It's downright subversive. It's so truthful that any day now I expect the Intellectual Storm Troopers who protect Israel to have it 'revised'.

DAILY/WEEKLY/MONTHLY Sources

◆ *Nation* is a weekly news magazine that is usually very close to true. *However*, it has a wide variety of writers (Alexander Cockburn & Christopher Hitchens; Edward Said & Noam Chomsky occasionally) who each have their own minds, and who, every now and then, go off the deep end and surprise you with unpredictable ideas.

◆ *Lies of Our Times* is a spunky little magazine devoted to helping us natives see through the tilt, spin, and trickery of *The New York Times*—and through the media knuckleballers in general.

◆ *Z Magazine* is the place where articles by Noam Chomsky regularly appear. Sorry to be redundant, but if you're unsure which version of a story is true, go with Chomsky. He does his homework, he's hard to fool, he's honest, and he's fair.

> NOTE: the fact that *The New York Times* is singled out for criticism may make you think that it's one of our *worst* newspapers; not true. *The NYTimes* is better than 99% of our newspapers & <u>all</u> TV news. *The NYTimes* is America's "newspaper of record", "all the news that's fit to print." The fact that *The NYTimes* is almost so good is part of what makes it so bad. The other part is, it seems so authoritative. (It's so grey it *must* be true, right?)

RADIO

◆ **WBAI, 99.5FM, New York:** their **News Reports** are unbeatable, as is their special coverage during times of crisis (like the Gulf War).

◆ Also on WBAI, check out **"Tahrir: Voices of the Arab World"**, hosted by **Barbara Nimri Aziz,** devoted to the radical premise that Arabs & Muslims are just plain folks like everybody else. If that simple truth was accepted, America would apologize to Iraq, terrorism would stop, and Israel would give back Palestine.

TV

In the beginning of this book I referred to a study that showed that the *more you watched TV* during the Gulf War, the *less you knew about the Gulf War.* That's no joke. How can that be? 'Disinformation.' The wrong information is worse than no information at all. (Speaking of Disinformation: there's a nice-looking, bald-headed, spiffy-dressing guy that CBS trots out as its Token AyRab. His name is Fouad Ajami and he's a real Uncle Tonoose. He hates Arabs, so naturally CBS loves him!)

PHOTOS

◆ *Palestine, a Photographic Journey* by **George Azar.** Elegant and harrowing photographs by a young Arab American who went to Palestine to capture the truth...and was almost killed for his trouble.

A Partial Bibliography

American Arab Affairs. Quarterly. Washington, DC: American-Arab Affairs Council.

Arendt, Hannah. *On Violence.* New York: Harcourt, Brace & Jovanovich, 1969.

Arendt, Hannah. *Eichmann in Jerusalem.* NY: Penguin, 1963.

Begin, Menachem. *The Revolt.* NY: Dell, 1951.

Bellow, Saul. *To Jerusalem and Back.* New York: Viking Press, 1976.

Ben-Asher, Naomi & Leaf, Hayim, edited by. *The Junior Jewish Encyclopedia.* New York: Shengold Pub., 1961.

Benziman, Uzi. *Sharon, an Israeli Caesar.* Tel Aviv: Adam Publishers, 1985.

Chomsky, Noam. *The Fateful Triangle.* Boston, MA: South End Press, 1983.

Chomsky, Noam. *Necessary Illusions.* Boston, MA: South End Press, 1989.

Chomsky, Noam & Herman, Edw.S. *Manufacturing Consent.* NY: Pantheon, 1988.

Chomsky, Noam. *Pirates & Emperors—International Terrorism in the Real World.* Brattleboro, VT: Amana Books, 1986.

Committe to Protect Journalism. *Journalism Under Occupation: Israel's Regulation of Palestinian Press.* NY & London: CPJ,1988

Congressional Quarterly. *The Middle East, 7th ed.* Washington, DC:Congressional Quarterly, 1991.

Emerson, Gloria. *Gaza—a Year in the Intifada: a Personal Account of an Occupied Land.* NY: Atlantic Monthly Press, 1991.

Encyclopedia Britannica, The. subjects: Palestine; Israel; Ancient Israel; Judaism;

Frankel, William. *Israel Observed.* NY: Thames & Hudson,1980.

Friedman, Thomas L. *From Beirut to Jerusalem:* New York, Doubleday, 1989.

Gilbert, Martin, Consulting Editor. *The Illustrated Atlas of Jewish Civilization.* New York: Macmillan, 1985.

Goldschmidt, Jr., Arthur. *A Concise History of the Middle East.* Boulder, CO.: Westview Press,1976,1991.

Gonick, Larry. *The Cartoon History of the Universe.* New York: Doubleday, 1990.

Green, Stephen. *Taking Sides—America's Secret Relations with a Militant Israel.* Brattleboro,VT: Amana,1988.

Gresh, Alain & Vidal, Dominique. *A to Z of the Middle East:* London, Zed Books, 1990.

Grun, Bernard. *The Timetables of History: A Horizontal Linkage of People & Events.* N.Y.: Simon & Schuster, 1982.

Hayes, John. R., Ed. *The Genius of Arab Civilization: Source of the Renaissance.* New York: NYU Press, 1992.

Herman, Edward & O'Sullivan, Gerry. *The Terrorism" Industry.* NY: Pantheon, 1989.

Hiro, Dilip. *Inside the Middle East.* NY: McGraw-Hill, 1982.

Hunter, Jane. *Israeli Foreign Policy—South Africa & Central America.* Boston: South End Press: 1987

Joumblatt, Kamal. *I Speak for Lebanon.* London: Zed Press, 1982.

Journal of Palestine Studies, The. Quarterly. Berkeley, CA: The University of California Press..

Khoury, Elias. *Little Mountain:* Minneapolis, MN: Univ. of Minnesota Press, 1989.

Lamb, David. *The Arabs.* NY: Vintage Books, 1987.

Lamb, Franklin P, ed. *Israel's War in Lebanon: Eyewitness Accounts of the Invasion & Occupation.* Boston: SouthEnd Press,1984

Laquer, Walter & Rubin, Barry, ed. *The Israel-Arab Reader.* New York, Penguin Books, 1969.

Lewis, Bernard, Ed. *The World of Islam.* London: Thames & Hudson, 1976.

Mackey, Sandra. *Lebanon, Death of a Nation:* New York, Doubleday, 1989.

Makdisi, Jean Said. *Beirut Fragments: a War Memoir.* NY: Persea Books, 1990.

Matar, N.I. *Islam for Beginners.* NY: Writers & Readers Pub. Inc., 1992.

Metropolitan Museum of Art. *Treasures of the Holy Land: Ancient Art from the Israel Museum* [ref. to exhibit Sep86-Jn87.

Middle East Journal, The. Quarterly. Washington, DC: The Middle East Institute.

Morse, Arthur D. *While Six Million Died.* Woodstock, NY.: Overlook Press, 1967.

Murphey, Cecil B., compiled by. *Dictionary of Biblical Literacy.* Nashville, TN: Oliver Nelson Books, 1989.

Murphy, Jay, ed. by. *For Palestine.* NY: Writers & Readers, Publishing, Inc., 1993.

Nassib, Selim with Tisdall, Cariline. *Beirut: Frontline Story.* Trenton, NJ: Africa World Press, 1983.

O'Heffernan, Patrick. *Mass Media & American Foreign Policy.* Norwood, NJ: Ablex Pub., 1991.

Ostrovsky, Victor & Hoy, Claire. *By Way of Deception.* NY: St. Martin's Press, 1990.

Peretz, Don. *Intifada.* Boulder, CO: Westview Press, 1990.

Ramsey Clark & Others. *War Crimes: a Report on U.S. War Crimes Against Iraq.* Wash.DC: Maisonneuve Press,1992.

Randal, Jonathan C. *Going All the Way: Christian Warlords, Israeli Adventurers & the War in Lebanon.* NY:Vintage,1984.

Safran, Nadav. *Israel, the Embattled Ally.* Cambridge, Mass.:Belknap Press of Harvard U. Press, 1978.

Said, Edward W. *Orientalism.* NY: Vintage, 1978.

Said, Edward W. *Covering Islam.* NY: Pantheon, 1981.

Said, Edward W. *The Question of Palestine.* NY: Vintage, 1979.

Said, Edward W. & Hitchens, Christopher, Ed. *Blaming the Victims.* London: Verso, 1988.

Schiff, Ze'ev & Ya'ari, Ehud. *Israel's Lebanon War.* New York: Simon & Schuster, 1984.

Spanier, John. *American Foreign Policy Since World War II.* Wash.DC: Congressional Quarterly, 1991.

Szlakmann, Charles. *Judaism for Beginners.* NY: Writers & Readers Pub. Inc., 1990.

Timerman, Jacobo. *Prisoner without a Name, Cell without a Number:* New York, Vintage Books, 1982.

Timerman, Jacobo. *The Longest War—Israel in Lebanon:* New York, Vintage Books, 1982.

Yermiya, Dov. *My War Diary—Lebanon: June 5-July 1, 1982.* Boston: South End Press, 1983.

Index